# P L A Y S

## 1 9 9 6 – 2 0 0 0

# P L A Y S

## 1 9 9 6 - 2 0 0 0

## RICHARD MAXWELL

THEATRE COMMUNICATIONS GROUP / NEW YORK / 2004

# CONTENTS

# CHAMPIONS
# OF MAGIC

*Champions of Magic* premiered at the Ontological Theater in New York City in May 1996. Direction by the author. Original cast:

Bob Feldman

So, it's an "old school" reunion with all the great magicians—well we weren't called that back then. Back then we were "conjurors." Anyway, at the table are James Carl, Burling Hull, Harlan Tarbell and George Schulte and myself. Along with Copperfield and Gallup. We're all sitting having a nice dinner. And Gallup starts to loosen up a bit and anyway starts to brag about how much he pulled in for two weeks at Merv Griffin in Atlantic City. He's going on and on about six figures this, six figures that, and a 110 profit margin and it's—well, it's embarrassing. Everyone is very uncomfortable. We're looking down at the table waiting, hoping this guy will shut his mouth. Except George. George, without any warning, he starts doing Gallup's money conversion trick. Not only is he doing it, but he's revealing. So as Gallup is blathering on unaware, his best trick is being exposed in front of everybody!

So everybody starts laughing and Gallup of course thinks he's the life of the party. But the funniest part is that while everyone at the table is busting a gut—Copperfield is turning red 'cause he's ticked-off. He doesn't like what's happening at all. So he gets up, throws his napkin on the table and leaves in a huff. And poor Gallup doesn't know what he's said to make him so upset. Meanwhile the rest of us are crying. Crying!

\* \* \*

Before proceeding with my performance, I will first roll up my sleeves—magicians and politicians are usually suspected of having something up their sleeve. So they have—their arms—but that's a birthday present. The magical effect I am about to present, has mystified and amused thousands of hi-brows, lo-brows and no-brows. That Robert Gallup isn't doing anything that hasn't been done before. Y'know I met Robert Gallup. I mean, total fake. The guy doesn't know what he's doing. Thinks he's some kind of Houdini. It's all smoke and mirrors. No class. No finesse. First of all, real magic doesn't do that. It doesn't have to. What these guys don't understand is the state of mind. And I don't get the TV thing at all. TV . . . don't get me started. I mean, let's talk about real magic for a second. Real magic is, is watching baby take its first step. Real magic is watching a beautiful girl on a hot day walk down the street. Or suddenly realizing that you have the ability to make someone smile. None of these guys understand this. Copperfield, Gallup, they don't understand. People want to believe you when you have the proper state of mind.

\* \* \*

You know, I have a trick I do. It's wonderful. I can't show it to you. But, it's amazing. I can only show you the inner part of it. The inner mechanism. To do the whole package would be too much for this place. I mean this place is small. I'm used to much bigger places. Auditoriums . . . The Hard Rock Hotel in Las Vegas . . . The Long Beach Civic Arena . . . Nassau Coliseum. 40-hundred plus. This trick would probably blow this place up. Seriously. No, it's too much . . . we'll see. I could hurt you. Maybe'll show you.

\* \* \*

A lot of times I'm asked to give advice to the young, aspiring magicians—I just have one thing to say: practice, practice, practice. You know, I once knew this little kid who had one card trick and a dirty little card table that he set up on the street for spare change. Folks would stop and watch. If they had time—sometimes they wouldn't stop—but if they did and they liked it, they would maybe throw a quarter in the cup. Or a dime. Or a nickel. Or whatever change they had in their pocket. Anyway, this kid worked real hard and sometimes would come home with a couple dollars. And he would get real discouraged. But, he never gave up, he never quit trying. And finally one day that little boy got the call to appear on *The Johnny Carson Show* and that was that. He went on to become a wildly successful magician. And do you know who that magician is today? . . . It's me. *(Pause)* I'm very successful.

# BILLINGS

*Billings* premiered in 1996 at the Williamstown Theatre Festival in Williamstown, MA. Direction by the author. Lights by Ian Claridge. Original cast:

| | |
|---|---|
| MAN | Josh Stamberg |
| WOMAN | Beata Fido |
| MOVER #1 | Christopher Fitzgerald |
| MOVER #2 | Sam Wright |
| MOVER #3 | Pete Simpson |

In 1997 it was performed at the Ontological Theater in New York City. Lights by Jane Cox. Costumes by Mattie Ullrich. Change in cast:

| | |
|---|---|
| MOVER #1 | Kevin Hurley |
| MOVER #2 | Lakpa Bhutia |
| MOVER #3 | Gary Wilmes |

# 1          THE FIRST HOUSE

*A room with furniture. A Man stands in the room facing the audience. His Wife stands to the far side of the room, looking at the Man, waiting. After a time, three Movers wearing Minnesota Vikings jackets enter the room.*

MAN: How are you?
#1 MOVER: Everything goes?
WIFE: Yes.

*The men move furniture out of the room.*

MAN: I like Billings all right. But I think I got a better thing in Minneapolis . . . It's pretty good. Yeah. It's a good job. I do all right. We should do all right. It's hard work though. I don't know if you've ever done this kind of thing before but it's pretty hard to do. I work a lot . . .

But I make my own hours which is good. Yeah . . . A lot of people are moving out to Minneapolis. A lot of people I know. Ha-ha. You guys must be busy I know so many people!

Yeah . . . I don't know, though. Billings is nice. Billings, Montana. I moved out to Billings in the fall of 1994 with a friend from high school, Jim McQuillan. I had two jobs: Elmer's Steakhouse and the Paddle Wheel Casino. At Elmer's Steakhouse I was a day host and at the Paddle Wheel Casino, I was a bartender.

There are lots of places to eat. It's pretty convenient. Lots of nice people. Everything is pretty close, so . . . I like it.

The weather is cold sometimes. But fall and spring are really nice. Great seasons. And you really get all four seasons in Billings.

—But Minneapolis is good, too. I mean a lot of the same things could be said about Minneapolis. There you got lots of nice places to eat. Plenty of things to do . . . It's very exciting. I think I'm going to like Minneapolis.

I got this pamphlet from the Chamber of Commerce.

*Looks at pamphlet. Long pause while the Man rolls his eyes up to think.*

What else, what else . . . The scenery here I might miss. That could be the hardest part. Leaving the scenery. I mean if you look out that window you see some amazing things out there. I don't know if I'd have the same thing in Minneapolis. It would be different, that's for sure.

I try to think about what it looks like there. I try to picture it in my mind . . . It's hard. I see lots of tall buildings. I wonder if that's right. I see lots of streets. I see lots of lights. I wonder if that's right.

I guess we'll just have to wait and see . . . ha-ha.

*The Movers enter again and approach the Man.*

#2 MOVER: We're tired. Did you know that? We would like to sit outside on the stoop and rest.

*Pause.*

MAN: What are you asking me?

*Pause.*

#1 MOVER: We worked very hard. We had to get up early. Probably earlier than you.

*Pause.*

MAN: I don't know what you want.

#1 MOVER: We're going outside. You have a lot of furniture, dude.

*The Movers exit.*

MAN *(To the Movers)*: I guess you'll go out to Minneapolis and then I guess probably you'll come back here. I don't suppose you'll stay in Minneapolis.

*The room is now empty of all furniture. The Man looks at the Wife.*

WIFE: Grandpa built this house five years ago. He was a drunk and he built very poorly. The wind would whip through the house in the winter and in the summer the bugs would crawl in and bite you while you slept. The first year he grew wheat. It was a wet year. He made some money. When the ground was soil you could make some money. But, the next year, it rained too much and the soil turned to mud. More bugs. Large ponds formed in the fields. We didn't have any money. And then it happened again. Rain and more rain. The mud was all we had. Nothing grew. He started going around to all the neighbors asking them for food. It was embarrassing. He started selling pieces of the house. The money he made he spent on booze and alcohol. Soon we had half a house and no food, no friends. That winter was one of the coldest ever . . . We lived day to day not knowing what disaster would come next. I remember after that it was very difficult being around him.

*Wife sings:*

> This house has many corners
> Some are square
> And some are not
> In this corner there lies
> 12 things that I'd forgot

> It makes me sad
> To leave this place
> I had a life
> And all of that

> Listen to your house
> You'd be surprised
> I'm talking about my house
> You'd be surprised

> I was surprised

> This house has many corners
> Some were hidden until now.

*They exit.*

# 2                                    THE JOURNEY

*An Amtrak train. We hear the sound of it rolling over the tracks from inside. In the foreground is the couple from Scene 1. They are sitting together looking out the window. In the background are the three Movers from Scene 1. They appear to be asleep.*

MAN: What time is it? . . .

WIFE:

MAN: You know what? The alarm on my watch went off. I didn't think my watch had an alarm on it. It's strange. I thought I owned an analog watch. It's weird being on this train. I don't like it I don't think.

*Pause.*

Are you hungry? I'm going to get something. Do you want anything?

WIFE: No thanks.

MAN: I'm hungry . . . What are you doing?

WIFE: I'm getting up.

MAN: I thought you said you weren't hungry.

WIFE: I'm going to use the bathroom.

MAN: *I'm* hungry.

*They both exit. Pause. The Movers in back begin to stir. #1 Mover looks at #3 Mover, then speaks:*

#1 MOVER: I don't like Mike anymore. He's not like he used to be. He's with those people who think they're so important. And they work with hunched backs and squinty eyes. I don't like that. They look like animals. They never bathe, C.J. . . . They make lots of money. So much money and they act like animals. He thinks he's great. I don't see what's so great about that. Mike . . .

#2 MOVER: Yeah.

#1 MOVER: He doesn't even need to do the moving gig. He could quit it. I mean, I wouldn't be surprised . . . He could just stay in that office, looking like an animal. Or an ape.

#2 MOVER: It's true.

#1 MOVER: Yeah . . . It is true. He looks like a caveman! Ha-ha!

*Pause.*

Look at this guy . . . Y'know what, y'know what's amazing
to me—how come this dude makes so much money? . . . He
makes a lot of money. They all do. How can he make so much
money and still look so disgusting? How is that? He should
go work for that other dude. Seriously. They don't give a shit
how they look and they don't bathe. How is it they make all
the money? Think about it—a 100,000 dollars. I don't get it.
They look like animals, dude. I'm serious. You know?!

#2 MOVER: Uh-huh.

#1 MOVER: He's in that office. And he types. He types. That's all
he does. And he's sitting down. So think about it. He wakes
up in the morning, rolls out of bed, throws on clothes that
he wore yesterday, and goes to work without a shower, without shaving, dude, walks to work and takes the elevator to
the office and sits down with a cup of coffee. It's a joke.
Seriously, dude.

#2 MOVER:

#1 MOVER: And look at what we do. We wake up early and we
shower and shave. We wait for the bus. It takes us a long
time to get to work. And we get to work and we go to work.
6 days a week. It hurts your back and hurts your legs. Early
in the morning before anyone else, we gulp our coffee and
it burns our tongue. We swallow our donuts whole while we
work. The both of us. While he goes in there, munchie
munch, you know—like an ape—and looks at a secretary's
ass. This really makes me angry.

*Pause.*

I don't want to talk about it anymore. You know what I'd
like to talk about instead? I'd like to talk about tomorrow.
The main thing is the game tomorrow. I like thinking about
that. That's what matters.

#2 MOVER: Yeah, that's important. I like thinking about that, too.

#1 MOVER: You know what? I feel this could be it. I feel so good
about this year. —You know, I wouldn't tell you this, but it

played out so good last week that I cried. No kidding. And you know what, I'm not ashamed to admit that.

#2 MOVER: What?

#1 MOVER: Cried, dude.

#2 MOVER: Is that true? Did you really cry?

#1 MOVER: I really did.

*Pause. #3 Mover wakes up.*

#3 MOVER: Where are we?

#1 MOVER: Detroit Lakes.

#3 MOVER: Is that all?

#1 MOVER: Yeah, dude.

#3 MOVER: I thought we were further than that.

#1 MOVER: You fell asleep.

*The Man and Wife come back to their seats. They have snacks.
They sit and begin to eat.*

WIFE: Mother was an odd creature. She worked at the Red Robin Hotel in Billings for 32 years. In the '80s the most she ever made was about 3 dollars an hour. She worked about 70 hours a week. I remember every night she would come home and just fall on the bed and I would have to undress her. She never ate. At least I never saw her eat.

In the morning, before work, I would ridicule her by quizzing her on current events. She had not a clue what was going on in the world. She didn't know anything. She said she didn't have time. Sometimes the teasing would become so intense that she would plead with me to stop. I never let up and often I would send her to work hysterically crying. I'll never forget those days. Those were tough times . . .

*The Movers take turns talking.*

#1 MOVER: I like alcohol. For 3 reasons. I got drunk last night. It helps me think. And it's a part of history. First, this dude

I knew says that it helps him think because it clears his head. I agree with that. Second, last night I had a good time because that dude from across the street brought over a case. Third, it was something that was always there . . . I know my old man drank it. And his old man before that, so, yeah, it was always a part of history.

#3 MOVER: I like pornography. My ex old lady hates it and she looks like porn. I don't have to buy it. I don't like to talk when I have sex.

My ex old lady hates it. But I don't care. She looks like she came out of one of those. I like a woman with a nice, high, tight ass.

If I go in over there, I don't have to buy the shit, I just pick it up and look at it. Every day I do that and Mohammed isn't going to do anything about it.

I also, sometimes I don't want to talk when I'm doin it. That's a real bitch. Saying that shit to your lady: "Ohh. Ohh. Oh." All that.

#2 MOVER: I don't like him. *(Indicates the Man)* He doesn't have the right attitude. He only cares about himself. If he got stupid, I'd get violent on his ass. Number 1: You can tell where he's from. He's clean. You know he's got money coming from something. Look at his clothes. Number 2: He came here with nothing to say to anybody except when he needed something. And Number 3: If it came down to it, and he's walking down the street, he looks at me stupid, or he says something, I will mess him up. Crack. Fuck. You go for the knees. These kids go for the head. Grab the knees, dude. So, I said, he's not like us. He only cares about himself. And if he got stupid, I'd get violent on his ass.

WIFE: My son who had bad feet. I couldn't say what it was, but I think it was rickets, or gangrene, something—one of those 19th-century diseases. His feet had grown to grotesque proportions. And they caused him great pain. At first he could walk a little bit, with a limp but then it got worse. And before long, he took to crawling. And finally the pain became so great that all he could do was writhe around on the ground. He was so miserable that he considered taking a leave of absence from his job. He was reluctant because he didn't know how he would be able to afford not working. He was able to convince his manager to loan him 20 dollars for food which he had to have delivered, leaving him about 10 dollars for the week . . . It was a struggle but he was able to pull through on a 50-pound bag of puffed rice . . . I know this sounds incredible but it really did happen. He was lucky. Some stories don't end that happy . . .

*#3 Mover stands up at his seat and begins to sing:*

#3 MOVER:
      15 years ago
      We had Bud Grant
      We had Chuck Foreman, and
      Fran Tarkenton

      And you're saying
      Had it been different
      Our team would be better

      Divine unsettlement
      Holds us in a trance
      Today we're not going to stand
      For flimsy circumstance

      Green grid iron
      Nature and rings
      These are a few of my favorite things

      Let's say you had 9 lives
      And you're on the 4th
      What I want to know is
      Would you take that chance?

*The Man is looking out the window.*

MAN: I don't know about this. I don't know. I feel so strange.
We're on the train now, but we'll be in Minneapolis very
soon. My stomach hurts. It feels all knotted.

## 3                                          THE NEW HOUSE

*The new house in Minneapolis. It is half the size of Billings. The
Man and his Wife walk in, looking around at the empty sur-
roundings. Soon, the Movers enter with furniture. They configure
the furniture to the new house. When they are finished, the furniture makes it impossible to move.*

MAN: Okay. This is interesting . . . I've never seen this (place)
before. This is new. This isn't like the other place. Okay . . .
I see. This isn't like Billings. It's different. I might like this.
Do I like this? Yeah . . . yeah, I think I do. So many things
to look at. I bet there are a lot of rooms. Different rooms.
You know, this is kind of how I pictured it . . . *(Looks at Wife)*
    Let me look out the window . . . Oh. This is interesting.
Wow. I see the uh, building across the way. It has a fire
escape. Yeah. We must be high up. *(Looks up)* Oh, look.
Wow. Okay. I'm starting to get the feel for this place. It
might take some getting used to. I see. Well, what do you
know. This is, okay . . . I think I know what this is. Good . . .
There's the light.
    This must be the kitchen . . . There's something different
about this kitchen . . . something's missing . . . I wonder
what it is . . . No stove. I wonder if I'll need a stove . . .
    It'll be strange calling this place "home." —It might take
a while to get used to, because in my head I'll mean the
other place. But . . .

I've seen so many things over the last few days. It's been incredible. It's been a really interesting experience. First, the train. Now this. Minneapolis. Minneapolis will be completely different.

*The Movers finish moving and approach the Man.*

#2 MOVER: Did you know that we have to go? I was wondering if we could get paid. Do you think we could get paid? I want you to write us a check now.

MAN: I'd like to pay you but my wife has the checkbook. *(He writes them a check)*

WIFE: Something happened around 1976. I discovered I had a spiritual side. I came to the conclusion that I had the supernatural capacity to communicate with the likes of Krishna, Mohammed, Buddha, Jesus, Allah, David, Pan . . . *(She turns to the others)* Watch me. I would take long walks. I read a lot. Learned a lot . . . It got pretty feverish. You've heard of speaking in tongues? I had all of that. I have experienced that spiritual ecstasy many times. I have had several epiphanies. At one time I was an active member of three places of worship. You don't understand my spirituality. It is very complex. I had people come up to me and ask *me* the way toward enlightenment.

I shouldn't say this—it isn't that I'm being rude—but don't ever accuse me of being secular, or lacking passion, or not doing my duty when it comes to these things. I know what I'm doing. I used my eyes to see the things that most people cannot. I have done so many things unthanked. Unnoticed. I don't need to mention them. I don't need to . . . but I did it. I did it.

*The Movers come center stage. Music begins. As the Movers leave the house, the couple begins small talk, under the music. The Movers sing:*

THE MOVERS:
> There are not a lot of things we can enjoy
> There are not a lot of things we can afford
> But there exists one pleasure for us
> We just got paid
> We are headed to the game
> We will sit and we will stand
> I'm sure you've seen us on TV

*(They sing the chorus:)*

> Before the Dome
> We took our shirts off
> It was 20 below
> You might have seen us.

*The Movers are joined by the couple for the last chorus.
Repeat ad nauseam.*

# SUPERINTENDENTS

*Superintendents* premiered at the Ontological Theater in New York City in May 1997. Direction by the author. Original cast:

Jose Nunez
Kevin Hurley
Warren Avery
Ellen LeCompte
Peter J. Coriaty

*5 people enter and stand in a line facing the audience.*

This is Jose Nunez. I'm at 339 W. 38th Street. People know it 'cause it's right near Penn Station. I have 52 1-room efficiencies. That's a lotta 'partments. 7 floors. You know I'm always goin round cleanin up there. Stairs. They ain't got no elevator. I mean there's an elevator but it don't work. I keep tellin him they gotta fix it—you know they got old ladies in there. They can't keep climbin those stairs. I have a pretty good lock on the apartments . . . tight . . . You know, no drugs, no booze. No kids smokin on the stoop. It wasn't always that way. It used to be a whole different thing. I remember chasin you know, pros out of there. That used to be all like trees over there next to it. We'd go in there an' chase em out. We'd get flashlights and shine em on them. And, there would be these Mexicans who lived in the building next door. And they would be rude to ladies. So me and Frankie, and this other dude went over there when they were sittin outside there gettin drunk and we kicked the shit out of them. I went up to that one dude an fuckin pow. I knocked him down . . . Yeah. But it's totally different around there now. Good people. Working. I got nice apartments there. Real nice apartments.

\* \* \*

I'm mechanic at 134, 136, 138 and ah, 140 W. 109th . . . yo. It's 4 buildings. It's a lot of apartments. Put it this way. The amount of garbage that these buildings put out, could fill a roll-off dumpster in one day. One day, dude. I got a deal with my land-

lord too. I don't pay rent. Basically. I was rent-control before
that. So, yeah, it was my mother's apartment. But now she lives
in Texas with my stepfather. Put it this way. Yo. My rent was so
low before, that my landlord would have to pay me for doing all
the work . . . He wasn't about to do that! . . . I can tell you that!
Now I spend my check on things that make my life a little easier.
I like to party . . . I can party all night and still wake up in the
morning and go to work. Yo. That's how it is. Some people can
swing with that. I guess it's a question of how much you can take,
dude . . . My old lady, she lives with me in the apartment . . .
sometimes she helps with taking out the garbage. Which is
good. I like the way she looks though, dude. Her ass could kill
you. A great ass, dude. Put it this way. You would look at her ass
and you'd think, "Yo. I sure would like to knock off a piece of
that ass." Straight up. Yeah. I like to watch this one girl in that
apartment below me through the airshaft—she doesn't know.
So, that's pretty good. Yeah . . .

* * *

I only have 1 building. It's interesting because I never really envi-
sioned myself becoming the super. How I fell into becoming the
super is that the landlord of my building called me 6 years ago
and told me that the original super had passed on. I knew who
he was. His name was Jimmy. Anyway, he asked would I be
interested in being the super for my building. I said I would have
to think about it. I thought about it and came up with an answer
for him within 24 hours. I decided I would do it. The reason
I decided I think was because I thought about the compensation
reduction in my rent I would get each month for the chores that
I would do. You don't know what those chores are, well, let me
tell you: I have to sweep the floors twice a week, mop the floors
(when it isn't rainy weather) once a week. Take out the garbage
3 times a week and the recycling 2 times a week. If any tenant
has any problem with something going wrong in their apartment, I will go and look at the problem and try to decide if
I could fix it. If I can fix it, I'll try and fix it right then. If I can't

fix it, I'll call the landlord and he'll send someone out. Usually Rey. Well. Those are pretty much my duties. I enjoy it given that I'm on disability. It does keep me pretty busy.

\*  \*  \*

My name is Lucy. I work at 524 W. 49th Street. You know, I was speaking to that nice lady who used to live on 48th Street. I was speaking with her just today and she was saying that all the people in her building had to move back down to 48th Street from up across the street from me. In 1 week. They used to be over there. But the city told them they have to move, "no" because they were fixing that building up. It's a city building. I said did you know you had to move so soon? And she said that she did, and I said Oh. They had told her but that she didn't know it would be so soon. I said wasn't that hard with your family to move like that back and forth for such a short time? And she said no it wasn't too bad. I said what about your family, your babies? She said they all helped. I said Oh . . . I thought it would be hard with your whole family to move like that. My daughter lived in one of those city buildings. I thought it was horrible. They were never clean. One time I asked my daughter don't you get sick of this building being so dirty? And she said no, Mom, I'm used to it. I said Oh . . . I keep my building so clean. My tenants are like Oh, Lucy, you work so hard. Like that one man, How do you keep the building so clean? And I tell him, I don't like it when things are dirty. I say to them, Do you like it when your apartment is dirty? And he said, My apartment's always dirty. And I said Oh.

\*  \*  \*

I don't know. I've been in the super business for 25 years. My old man was a super. He handed down the job to me. I've had a problem with the drink, and I go back to the Salvation Army for a year this year. It seems like everyone around me is a drunk. I like to say I'm recovered, but I can't, quite frankly. I don't know what will happen to my building when I leave. Quite frankly,

I don't do much for it. You know people are always complaining . . . They got roaches, or rats, mice, their shower don't work. But—I tell them, this is a big city, and it costs money to fix things up. I tell you that their landlord ain't gonna pay to fix it, I'm not gonna pay to fix it. You fix it. Buy traps. I don't know. They shouldn't get angry. Quite frankly, I don't blame them though. I could take out the garbage better but I'm having trouble getting out of bed. Maybe when I leave, they can get somebody better. When I come back after a year, it might be better. Who'll say it'll be better. Who can say I'll want to do it still in a year. I might get something better. Quite frankly.

*Music. They sing "The More We Get Together."*

# FLIGHT COURIER SERVICE

*Flight Courier Service* premiered in 1997 downstairs at the Ontological Theater in New York City. Direction by the author. Costumes by Sibyl Kempson. Original cast:

| | |
|---|---|
| RENE | Josh Stamberg |
| CAROLYN | Kate Gleason |
| STEWARDESS | Kate Walsh |
| LAKPA | Lakpa Bhutia |
| MR. FELDMAN | Bob Feldman |

It was later performed upstairs. Lights by Jane Cox. Change in cast:

| | |
|---|---|
| STEWARDESS | Jennifer Krasinski |

**1**

*The stage is empty. A man enters.*

RENE: I'm in my apartment. I found a pamphlet. This looks
    interesting. "Have you ever thought about becoming a flight
    courier? Be an international flight courier." This sounds
    good. Hello? I called to learn about what it takes to become
    a flight courier.

PHONE: Hello?

RENE: Hellо.

PHONE: Couriers International, this is Carolyn. Can I help you?

RENE: Yes. I'm calling to be a flight courier.

PHONE: I'll send you our brochure if you like. What is your
    address please?

RENE: Um, I already have the, I think I have the brochure, actu-
    ally. I was wondering about—

PHONE: You already have the brochure . . . You've read the
    brochure?

RENE: Yes.

PHONE: Okay, tell me, can you tell me about yourself.

RENE: Yeah, actually.

PHONE: How did you find out about Couriers International?

RENE: Uh, I was looking at one of your magazines and I just saw
    an ad—

PHONE: What are you looking for?

RENE: What am I looking for?

PHONE: Yes, where would you like to go?

RENE: Um, oh. I don't know. I would enjoy flying. I'm ready to go to new places. I've had it with my life here, you know. I . . . don't really have an income right now, actually.

PHONE: Well, we don't pay you very much. You're given discounted airfare . . .

RENE: But, I'd like to try—I'm looking for work and I thought about trying other cities.

PHONE: Can you come in and fill out our application?

RENE: Okay, that'd be—okay.

PHONE: Come down to our office at 589 Madison Avenue and ask for Carolyn, okay? Mmmm. Bye.

RENE: 589, 589.


# 2

*The midtown office. Carolyn enters.*

RENE: Hello. I am Rene.

CAROLYN: Hi, you're here for the courier position? Okay, come on in, have a seat. I'm Carolyn. I spoke to you on the phone.

RENE: Oh. 'Cause your voice was familiar to me. Nice to meet you . . .

CAROLYN: Have you ever applied to a courier service before?

RENE: Well, I did work for like a messenger service once . . .

CAROLYN: Really?

RENE: It was CMC. It wasn't an airline. Ha, it was a bicycle messenger company. I's a bike messenger.

CAROLYN: We're an air courier service. Our priority is to provide a professional, individualized service. Fill out this application and we'll contact you within a week.

RENE: Ah . . .

CAROLYN: If accepted you'll be asked to check in once a week. Working for a courier means sacrificing certain things taken for granted. All our couriers must be available at all times. This means not being more than one hour from the airport at any time. Ah, no vacations, you can't take vacations . . . no out of town trips, no going home for the holidays.

RENE: Okay. Do you have an application or . . .

CAROLYN: We require all couriers to have proper attire to deliver packages. This means, for men, a nice, dark suit and a tie.

RENE: Uh . . . Okay . . . can I—

CAROLYN: Good. Let me have you fill out this.

RENE: . . . Thank you. Gimme—let me see your pen . . .

*He writes.*

I filled it out.

CAROLYN: All finished? Great. Thanks for coming in. If you don't hear from us within a week, give us a call.

# 3

*Rene's apartment.*

PHONE: Rene.

RENE: Hello?

PHONE: Rene?

RENE: Yes.

PHONE: Rene, it's Carolyn.

RENE: Carolyn who?

PHONE: I have some good news.

RENE: Okay . . . Oh!

PHONE: You're going to Asia. Are you ready? You leave today at
    6 A.M.

RENE: Today. Asia. Uh, okay . . . I just—

PHONE: You're going to Kuala Lumpur, Malaysia. For at least a
    couple weeks. We don't have a return flight for you yet. But
    the package is at our office where you'll pick up your itin-
    erary. An agent will escort you through to customs. And,
    don't forget your passport. Come down to the office. All
    right? Bye.

RENE: Right now? Man. What time is it?


# 4

*The midtown office. Rene enters.*

CAROLYN: Hi Rene. "Rene" . . . That's a strange name for a man,
    isn't it?

RENE: I don't know, ha!

CAROLYN: Are you French?

RENE: I'm 'merican! Actually, you know, I don't know. —I don't
    think . . .

CAROLYN: Okay, why don't you sit down, I need to brief you . . .

RENE: Okay.

CAROLYN: Territory, Blok 1, Tingkat 2–3, Pusat, Damansara,
    Bukit Damansara, 50490 Lumpur, tel: 03-2555077.
    Lumpur, Headquarters Office, Blok 1, Tingkat-7, Pusat
    Bandar Damansara, 50490 Kuala Lumpur, 03-2555077.
    Wisma Persekutuan Johor, Blok B, Tingkat, Jln Air Moick,
    80550 Johor Bahru, tel: 07-244255. Tingkat 2, Wisma
    Persekutuan, 0500 Alor Setar, tel: 04-733302. Tingkat 2,
    Wisma Persekutuan, Jln, 15550 Kota Bharu, Kelantan, tel:
    09-782644. Tingkat 2, Wisma Persekutuan, Hang Tuah,
    75300 Malacca, tel: 06-224958. Sembilan, Tingkat 2, Wisma

Persekutuan, Datuk Abdul Kadir, 70675 Seremban, Negri, tel: 06-714551. Tingkat 1, Wisma Persekutuan, Jln Gambut, Kuantan, Pahang, tel: 09-512155. Bangunan Persekutuan, Jln Dato'Panglima, Gantang, 30000 Ipoh, Perak, tel: 05-549316. Tingkat 1, Menara Kemajuan PKNP, JinLagi, 01000 Kangar, Perlis, tel: 04-762636. Pinang, Jln Leboh Pantai, 10550 Pinang, tel: 04-615122. Tingkat 4 & 5, Bangunan Penerangan, Kota Kinabalu, Sabah, tel: 088-216711. Peti Surat 639, 93908 Kuching, Sarawak: 082-245661. Kompleks PKNS, 40550 Shah Alam, tel: 03-5590653. Tingkat 1, Wisma Persekutuan, JlnBunya, 20200 Kuala Terengganu, Terengganu: 09-621424.

*Carolyn sings:*

> Tropical sun
> Laden with clouds
> Sudden downpour
> Kuala Lumpur
>
> Pornography
> Weapons and walkie-talkies
> Boil your water
> Don't be dehydrate
> Heavy rain, Kuala Lumpur.

# 5

*727 aircraft. Rene with package.*

STEWARDESS: Would you like something to drink?
RENE: What? Yes. Gimme—I want. —Can I get two things, actually?

STEWARDESS: I don't see why not.

RENE: I want a glass of orange juice and water. Do you have bottled water.

STEWARDESS: Well, it comes from the bottle.

RENE: Oh. But you can't give me the bottle?

STEWARDESS: Sure.

RENE: And a cup of ice—that's separate . . .

STEWARDESS: Okay . . .

RENE: Hey! I am Rene. I'm going to Malaysia. Can you believe it?

STEWARDESS: Well, that's great! Is this your first time, Rene?

RENE: Yes.

STEWARDESS: So, I take it you know Carolyn?

RENE: Yeah! How do you know her?

STEWARDESS: I see a few of Courier International people go through here. And this is where they seat you guys. They must have a high turnover over there? It's never the same person.

RENE: You're kidding. That's, that's amazing.

STEWARDESS: Yes . . . will Mr. Bhutia be meeting you at the airport when we get to Kuala Lumpur?

RENE: Yeah! Yeah, how do say his name?

STEWARDESS: Mr. "Boo-tee-ah."

RENE: Oh, 'cause I was wondering.

STEWARDESS: Yeah, he's nice, Mr. Bhutia. I like him. One time he had this party and he invited people from here, from work and I was the only one who showed up and he and I got to talking—turns out, he has a sister who used to work with me at another airline!

RENE: Yeah, I have this package to deliver. I wonder what it is? It feels like one of those computer things.

*He opens the envelope.*

STEWARDESS: Ooh. Are you supposed to do that?

RENE: I don't think it matters, actually.

STEWARDESS: Okay. Can I get you something else?
RENE: No, thanks. I'll—I won't sleep.
STEWARDESS: All right, then. Have fun in Kuala Lumpur!


# 6

*Rene at the airport in Kuala Lumpur.*

RENE: Look at this place!

*Lakpa Bhutia enters.*

LAKPA: Wow. Yeah. Hey. Your name is Rene, right?
RENE: Huh.
LAKPA: Yeah, hello, Rene, nice to meet you. Welcome to Kuala
    Lumpur.
RENE: That's right. Rene, yes.
LAKPA: My name is Lakpa. Lakpa Bhutia.
RENE: Lockbar?
LAKPA: Yeah, Lakpa it is. So, do you have the package?

*Rene hands Lakpa the package.*

All right. We'll take you to your hotel room. Hotel room, yeah.
RENE: I don't have a hotel room, actually.
LAKPA: Well, don't worry about it. Don't worry. We have a sur-
    prise for you. Mr. Feldman will take care of you. Mr. Feld-
    man would like to thank you for delivering his package. He
    has taken care of your lodging during your stay here in
    Kuala Lumpur, also.
RENE: He's going to pay for it?
LAKPA: Of course. In fact, Mr. Feldman is waiting for you in
    your room right now.
RENE: What's he doing in my room?

LAKPA: He just wants to make sure that you're comfortable. Really. So, relax! Yeah.

RENE: Lockbar, you're like those limousine drivers at airports who hold up signs. So this is Kuala Lumpur!

# 7

*Mr. Feldman in Rene's hotel room. Lakpa and Rene enter.*

LAKPA: Mr. Feldman, this is Rene.

MR. FELDMAN: Mr. Rene. Come in. How do you do.

RENE: Wow, you hardly have a accent at all, actually.

MR. FELDMAN: Thank you. Do you speak Malaysian?

RENE: Ha, no.

MR. FELDMAN: No? Chinese?

RENE: No.

MR. FELDMAN: Well, this visit might be hard for you. Forgive me, there's something I have to ask you.

RENE: Okay.

MR. FELDMAN: Do you know what was in the package that I had you deliver?

RENE: Uh . . . no.

MR. FELDMAN: Are you sure? The reason I ask you is that the package was opened somehow. I don't suppose anyone opened that package without you knowing about it?

RENE: No, see . . . I didn't.

MR. FELDMAN: I didn't think so. Since Carolyn has assured me that my courier will allow no one to tamper with my parcels. Carolyn is very careful to explain this is your responsibility. "It is the courier's responsibility to assure safe arrival once it has left the air." You remember that, right? So, now, are you telling me that the package was given to you like this, in this condition?

RENE: Well . . .

MR. FELDMAN: Yes?

RENE: Well, ask Carol maybe, I don't know—

LAKPA: He came off the plane with it that way.

MR. FELDMAN: Mr. Bhutia, you're interrupting Mr. Rene

LAKPA: I'm sorry, Mr. Rene.

MR. FELDMAN: Perhaps, Mr. Rene, you'd like to tell us what you really mean to say.

RENE: Okay, it's like this. See, I went through customs fine, but there was this agent who was with me and then this stewardess on the plane was like, "Hey what was in that package." And I's like, "I don't know. I'm a flight courier though." And she—she was like—she was doing her job, so I let her look at it. I mean, she saw it. And that was it. I mean that's how it happened, actually.

MR. FELDMAN: . . . Interesting. Okay . . . Now I understand. And all it will take is a phone call to Carolyn to clear this up. But I am confident that what you're telling me is the truth. Lakpa, let's let our guest retire. I know he'll want to rest in order to see all there is to see in Kuala Lumpur . . . You know we have the tallest building in the world now? Isn't that something? Good night, Mr. Rene.

*Mr. Feldman and Lakpa exit.*

RENE: No, I think the Sears Building is taller. In Chicago, actually. —Good night. Okay, I wonder what building he means . . . I'm excited to be in Kuala Lumpur, I guess. I mean it's everything Carol said it would be, actually . . . But, I feel that there's something weird going on. But then again, I get upset sometimes. No, that's not really true. I's pretty relaxed person I think, I mean. I don't know. It's strange because I'm not really sure how long I'm going to be here . . . It could be a month I guess. It could be a year. No, it won't be a year. Unless I get a job. That part is a little uncomfortable for me. Maybe I could work for Mr. Feldman. I could fill the time. Mr.

Feldman was right, there are a lot of things to do here . . . What a bright city . . . You know how some words come from some place else? Well, I think the word "pajamas" is Malaysian . . . Man, I'm thirsty. Carol was right about the dehydration. I guess I'm feeling it right now, actually. I need to get something from the vending machine.

*He goes into the hallway. Lakpa is standing outside. Rene closes the door.*

That guy Lockbar's out there. I think I really screwed this up. I should've never opened that package, actually.

*Rene runs to the window. Lakpa opens the door and catches him. Rene struggles free and escapes through the window.*

# 8

*The Stewardess enters.*

STEWARDESS: I'm close to thirty. No, damn, I can't lie like that—I'm thirty. And I was talking to a girlfriend who works with me on the plane the other day . . . She's married for about a year, and she's 3 months pregnant. I'm not sure, I'm guessing she's 25, 26. I think she's beautiful. She's glowing right now. Even though she smokes like a chimney and they're saying that's bad now when you're pregnant . . . I hate to admit it . . . I mean she looks so happy, I'm jealous of her. It's like, I think I want to have a child, too. I look around at all my friends and they have children, lots of children, and I'm thinking, What do I have? I have a crappy little room in Times Square that I see 3 days a week—if I can open my eyes for 2 seconds 'cause I'm sleeping the whole time I'm

there . . . I have a job that lets me eat 3 meals a day. But this
job takes up all my life on a plane to someplace in Asia
where I end up being 80 percent of the time. Living out of
a suitcase. I mean, no offense, but it's—I'll tell you the truth.
I hate Malaysia. What can I do? They have malls, but that's
it. What is there to do? How can it compare to this country?
I feel like it's a—it's like an imitation or something of the
real thing. I'd have more respect for the place if they had
some like dignity. Or even gave women some dignity. But—
or like a culture and a history they could remember or call
their own, but it's like it doesn't mean anything unless it
came from America. So, why live in a imitation . . . That girl
I was talking about before who's pregnant? She lives in
someplace outside of Kuala Lumpur. Damansara? I can't
remember, she lives there with her husband in a, sure it's a
nice house, but, what is it? It's cheap labor that's what it is.
Her husband gets a tax break through his job, and hires
people for 2 dollars a day. And she's like, "Yeah, we love it
in Asia. It's just like home, only we have all the things we
can't get in the States 'cause we can't afford it." She has all
the shit your parents had 30 years ago, but she had to go to
Southeast Asia to get it . . . So, anyway, I don't know . . . But
I would like to have a baby. My own baby. I'd like that.
I wouldn't smoke cigarettes either, I can tell you that much.

*She exits.*

# 9

*Rene on the streets of Kuala Lumpur.*

RENE: I really don't know where I am. I hurt myself. I gotta call
     Carol. —The pay phones are different here . . . Hello, hello
     Carol?!

*Carolyn enters.*

CAROLYN: . . . This is Carolyn. Who's this?

RENE: . . . Rene!

CAROLYN: . . . Rene! How was your trip? Did you deliver—

RENE: Oh, pretty good!

CAROLYN: Did you deliver the package all right?

RENE: Uh—ah, yeah. Whoa. That's weird . . . There's a delay thing with this . . .

CAROLYN: What?

RENE: Yeah! I don't think there are any jobs for me here. Um. I want to come home now. Is there a flight for me today or tonight?

CAROLYN: That's great.

RENE: . . . There is?

CAROLYN: Yes!

RENE: What time?

CAROLYN: What time what?

RENE: When does the flight leave?

CAROLYN: What flight?

RENE: My flight home. My flight back!

CAROLYN: . . . Rene, no, we don't have anything right now. And we won't know anything until Saturday. Give me a call on Saturday. Do you need a place to store your luggage? Maybe you could rent a locker. Do they have lockers there?

RENE: Lockbar? Yeah, he's here . . . uh—

CAROLYN: Okay?

RENE: Well, I did what you asked. I'm pretty much done here. Can I—

CAROLYN: Rene, I have to go. Good luck.

*She exits.*

RENE: . . . Hello?

# 10

*Mr. Feldman and Lakpa are having coffee at the All Night Deli.*

MR. FELDMAN: You never told me, what happened in the hotel room?
LAKPA: Oh, I never told you? Yeah, I opened the door and I was trying to wrestle with him. And we wrestled and wrestled. And he broke free of me. Yeah. He's a lot stronger than me, I think. Also, he went to the window and . . . crawled out. Yeah. He crawled out of the window.
MR. FELDMAN: He overpowered you then?
LAKPA: Yeah. Exactly. He did. He overpowered me.
MR. FELDMAN: Oh. He didn't hurt you did he?
LAKPA: No, he didn't. I don't believe he hurt me. No.
MR. FELDMAN: Okay. Good.

# 11

*Rene on the streets of Kuala Lumpur.*

RENE: Man, I can't sleep! I can't stay awake! I just walk around.

*Stewardess enters.*

Stewardess. Stewardess! Hey!
STEWARDESS: Rene, hi! How are you?
RENE: Not too good. I haven't slept in a while.
STEWARDESS: Why, what time did you get up.
RENE: Get up? I didn't sleep last night, at all, actually.
STEWARDESS: Well I had to be up at 4 A.M.
RENE: What time did you go to sleep?

STEWARDESS: What? I don't know 12, 1. Only to get to the airport to find that my flight had been canceled. So I went
shopping. Look at all the stuff I bought.

RENE: Oh. How come your flight was canceled?

STEWARDESS: They're saying "mechanical error."

RENE: Because I was looking for a flight.

STEWARDESS: What's the matter—why are you wearing pajamas?

RENE: I told you I didn't sleep last night. And I haven't eaten.

STEWARDESS: What happened?

RENE: I was trying to find a place to rest between chases with
Lockbar and Mr. Feldman, and I came to this All Night Deli.
This city is unbelievable. It's like being on another planet or
something. Anyway, I think it was down around the
Chinatown part of town, actually. It was quiet. It was still
hot and muggy. It was hard to breathe. It was late. I's surprised to find anyplace open, actually . . . I had about 30,
um, sen on me and I was going to buy something to drink,
I was so thirsty. I's in the deli which is small. The place
smelled like cat. I was sticking my head inside the refriger-
ator door pretending to look for something I liked. I already
knew what I wanted, you know, but I's jes trying to get cool.
When I feel this feeling. And without knowing why I turn
around, and I see this little boy looking up at me with this
look of like—I think he's laughing 'cause I'm wearing pajamas. And he was like, "You look tired." And then he points
down to these stairs that I can't see where they go. And he
motions for me to follow him. I's like, "What dangers lurk
there." Actually . . . he led me down these rickety old stairs
and it was so dirty. And at the bottom of the stairs were
cardboard boxes. Soggy boxes—everywhere. The floor was
covered in water. The boy pulled on my hand and was like—
said it was okay. I stepped on water and my shoes started to
leak. My shoes started to leak and my toes were squishing.
The kid showed me inside one of the boxes they had. They
had in the boxes, they kept these little packages just like the
one I had on the plane, that I gave to Mr. Feldman. Boxes

and boxes of those packages. They had them all in one of those soggy boxes. He took one out and showed it to me. I said I didn't want it—the kid laughed. Then he pointed to pictures on the wall. He waded through the water and went back upstairs. And I just had to get out of there. I looked at the pictures on the wall—they were all of like Mr. Feldman and Lockbar. I went up the stairs and out onto the street. It was just nice to be away from that place, actually. I walked a ways and sat down on the pavement. After all that, I forgot to get a soda.

*Rene sings:*

> I don't want to get dehydrate, actually
> I'll boil my water then drink it
> If the weather's hot
> I'll drink water
> I don't want to drink it boiled still, actually
> I jes wait till it cools off.

I don't know. I have so many like questions in my head. Do you know any answers for me?

STEWARDESS: What? What answers?

RENE: We were on the plane. You knew all the answers on the plane, you knew who I was, you knew who Lockbar was . . . why don't you tell—

STEWARDESS: I told you, I knew a lot of couriers from Couriers International because they fly the same route every week, the same time, carrying the same packages to the same person . . . That's all. Why, will you stop trying to corner me?

RENE: Well I am sorry then, there has to be some reason why I can't sleep. I don't have my money, and . . . those guys want to kill me . . . You tell me.

STEWARDESS: Why don't you let me help you.

RENE: Okay. Gimme a flight out of here.

STEWARDESS: You don't have a return ticket?

RENE: No. Carol couldn't find me a ticket.

STEWARDESS: All right. Do you have a place to stay?

RENE: No. Not really. I's jes on the streets.

STEWARDESS: I'll see what I can do. Come on, you can come back to my place and get cleaned up and then we'll see about a flight back home. Will you help me with my boxes?

# 12

*The All Night Deli.*

MR. FELDMAN: Do you want to talk about how we met?

LAKPA: Sure.

MR. FELDMAN: You remember? I think it was . . . when did you start working for Richard Barber?

LAKPA: Oh, man. I think it was a long time ago. Like 1993? 4 years, 5 years, yeah . . .

MR. FELDMAN: Yeah, I think that's right. You were working at Paradice.

LAKPA: Paradice! That fucking place, man. I remember you came in and I was like who's this guy? And Laura would always, always give you coffee . . .

MR. FELDMAN: Coffee or tea.

LAKPA: . . . Yeah, tea. And I was like, "Who's this guy, you know, who stands at the counter and gets free coffee?" Yeah, I said to Laura, you know, this guy comes in here and never pays, yeah. Really. He never pays!

MR. FELDMAN: I remember that.

LAKPA: And she says that's my boyfriend! I was like, "That's your boyfriend!" I was . . . I couldn't believe it, really. I thought you were like John Ford Noonan and all these people who come and ask for free stuff, yeah.

MR. FELDMAN: Yeah.

LAKPA: And it was then that we—I—yeah, you would bring in your horn, also. So I knew you were a musician. And then we would talk about music. I would ask you questions about jazz. Yeah.

MR. FELDMAN: I was surprised with how much you know about jazz.

LAKPA: Oh, man! Listen to this guy! You—this guy says I know a lot about jazz!

MR. FELDMAN: So, what do you think? We should probably find that kid.

LAKPA: Yeah, when we find him, I'm gonna kill him.

# 13

*Stewardess's hotel room.*

RENE: Why don't you take off your underwear too. Make yourself more comfortable, actually. Ha!

STEWARDESS: If I take off my panties and bra, you mean?

RENE: Well, yeah.

STEWARDESS: Well, then I wouldn't have anything on would I Rene?

RENE: No, you wouldn't.

STEWARDESS: I'd be naked in other words.

RENE: That's what I's hopin.

STEWARDESS: You know, Rene, we barely know each other.

RENE: I was just going to say the same thing.

STEWARDESS: I find you very attractive. If I take off all my clothes, there'll be no stopping. Is that what you want?

RENE: I want to take off my pajamas now.

STEWARDESS: Here, let me do it.

## 14

*The All Night Deli.*

LAKPA: I took a vacation once, yeah. I run a restaurant now. And I had some time off, you know. Because I work hard. It's hard work running a restaurant, also. I been working there for a long time, from 1994, and before that I worked as a cook since 1982. And I took my first vacation since I started. I went down to the Philippines, Manila, it is, you know. And other islands around there. I went for 3 weeks. Man, that place is, like, so different. Really. Yeah, I went down to breakfast on my first day. And I was walking around the streets of Old Manila when I started to get hungry, you know? And I went into this cafe and I went up to the counter and there was this guy back there making coffee and cooking breakfast for everybody. And I went up to the counter and I told him what I wanted and I started to think, this guy is me. I am him. That's me doing my job, you know? But I'm on vacation. I'm ordering from him, yeah. It feels pretty good to order something when you're not working. And all of the sudden, I liked everything around me, I liked the clothes I was wearing. Beautiful. Beautiful day. Beautiful girls. I thought, man, I should do this more often. I knew it was going to be a good vacation. Yeah.

MR. FELDMAN: So, I found out where that kid's at.

LAKPA: Oh yeah? Where is he?

MR. FELDMAN: He's staying with that stewardess.

LAKPA: Oh, really? Yeah? How did you find that out?

MR. FELDMAN: You want to go over there right now? We could get over there now and get it over with.

LAKPA: Yeah. Now. You want to go now? Did the stewardess tell you? I know, because you were going to talk to her.

MR. FELDMAN: That's what I'm saying. I know where they're at. We should go over there.

LAKPA: You want to go over there now? Yeah, I can't go now. Maybe later. Maybe later on, yeah, but not now. I think I'm a little too tired right now.

MR. FELDMAN: Oh. We don't have to go now. We can go later on.

LAKPA: Yeah, I think that's better for me. Later is better.

MR. FELDMAN: Sure.


# 15

*Stewardess's hotel room.*

STEWARDESS: Are you going to stay for breakfast?

RENE: No, I should probably go.

STEWARDESS: Go? Where will you go?

RENE: I don't know, actually. Can we go to the airport?

STEWARDESS: No, I have to make some phone calls. Relax.

RENE: I guess I'll stay.

STEWARDESS: Stay. Did you enjoy last night?

RENE: Well, it was, yeah. It was ah, nice.

STEWARDESS: It was nice?

RENE: Stewardess, I'm still thirsty. Can I get some more water. Or juice. Something?

*Stewardess sings:*

STEWARDESS:
> My name is _____
> You see my _____ hair
> Sometimes I work
> Sometimes I sleep
> I'm not telling you
> Anything untrue

Don't worry
You haven't missed a thing
If I had something new
You would know.

*Mr. Feldman and Lakpa enter.*

RENE: Whoa! What's going on? You guys! —How did you know
I was here. You . . .

MR. FELDMAN: Your girlfriend told us. Wasn't that nice?

STEWARDESS: Yes, I set you up? Of course. You're an idiot.

MR. FELDMAN: What's the solution here. We have to kill you,
Rene.

RENE: What for? 'Cause I looked at that package?

MR. FELDMAN: It really doesn't matter. We don't take chances
here anyway. But Carol wasn't too pleased with my report
on you: you opened my package and then you lied to me
about it.

RENE: Oh, man.

LAKPA: How do you want to kill this fuckin guy?

RENE: Wait . . . Carol will know where I am—how will you get
away with it?

MR. FELDMAN: It's *Carolyn*. She knows all about it.

RENE: You guys are like a . . . racket. What?

LAKPA: You're pretty sharp, yeah. I want to kill this fuckin guy,
Bob . . .

MR. FELDMAN: We can't take the chance of letting these things
get into the open, no matter who you are.

RENE: Who was on the package, then?

MR. FELDMAN: Who? What are you talking about, who.

RENE: The thing that I brought you.

MR. FELDMAN: That's not a package, that's called a *disk*. That's
very important information. Centuries old. Ready, Lakpa?
I think we're through talking.

LAKPA: Yeah.

# 16

*The Stewardess and Rene are at the airport.*

RENE: What are you doing?

STEWARDESS: I'm saving your life.

RENE: But, I thought you were—

STEWARDESS: Shut up. Now listen to me. Mr. Feldman gave me a lot of money to bait you. I'm not going to lose it. I'm going to take you to the gate and we're going to board a plane back home. When we get to the gate, you're my husband, all right?

RENE: But—

STEWARDESS: If you want to get out of here, you'll listen to me. In order for you to get onboard this plane, you need to know one thing. You're my husband—that's all you need to know—that's your ticket out of here.

RENE: As long as—

STEWARDESS: Kiss me. There are a lot of people now who want to see us dead.

RENE: Yeah . . . Hey. What day is this?

STEWARDESS: Saturday. Why?

RENE: No, I's jes . . .

STEWARDESS: Wait here.

*She exits. Rene goes to use the phone.*

RENE: Hello, Carolyn?

CAROLYN: Yes, Rene.

RENE: Hi. Yeah. It's Saturday. I's calling to see if you had anything.

CAROLYN: No, sorry. Nothing yet. But keep trying. Call every week. I never know what's coming in from there to here.

RENE: Well, I don't really have to go home, though. Actually, do you have anything to anywhere else?

CAROLYN: I'll check . . . I have a flight that leaves tonight for Seoul, South Korea.

RENE: Okay. That sounds good.

CAROLYN: You might be there for a while. I never get anything coming out of there.

RENE: That's okay. It sounds pretty good.

CAROLYN: Rene.

RENE: Yeah?

CAROLYN: I got a report from Mr. Feldman.

RENE: . . . You did?

CAROLYN: Do you want to tell me what happened out there.

RENE: I don't—I delivered the package! Do you know who these guys are?

CAROLYN: I know that they're customers of Couriers International.

RENE: I know, but—

CAROLYN: Forget it, Rene. I'm going to let it go this time. But in the future you gotta be more careful. This is very important. Now go get packed. You'll pick up your package at a place called the All Night Deli. It's down there in Chinatown.

RENE: That place?

CAROLYN: Oh, good. You know it.

RENE: Well, yeah. Uh—

CAROLYN: Rene, we're sending you to Seoul, South Korea. Rene.

RENE: What?

CAROLYN: You have my love.

RENE: What? Oh. Wow. I don't have anything to pack, Carolyn. Wow. Soul. That's pretty good. I wonder what Soul will be like.

*He exits.*

# 17

*Mr. Feldman and Lakpa enter.*

MR. FELDMAN: Hi. I'm Bob Feldman and this is Lakpa Bhutia. At this point I'm supposed to play but tonight I've gotta cut it short. I gotta get to this other gig. I'm playing—you won't believe where I'm playing. I'm playing the VFW in Ozone Park. Yeah. I gotta go way out there. I can tell you I'm not too happy about that. I gotta get there for the last set. I'm subbing for a guy who's gotta get to a Latin gig. I would take a cab, except the cab fare would be more than I'll make . . . so, I'll take the number 7 train out there. Yeah, it's with the Lester Lanin Orchestra. You know he's got that big band thing he does. He's not bad if you heard him. He's a fair musician. He's got good instincts. He's not as good as me. No one's as good as me . . . The number 7. I wonder how long I'll wait for that . . . Sometimes when I wait, I'll just play on the platform at 42nd Street without opening my case. They think I'm a street musician. They come over . . . looking—Germans mostly. Ha ha ha. And then they look at you—you know, "What are you doing? You're not begging for money." They can't believe it. Ha ha ha.

*He plays.*

# BURGER KING

*Burger King* premiered in 1997 at the Williamstown Theatre Festival in Williamstown, MA. Direction by the author. Original cast:

| | |
|---|---|
| DONALD | Christian Lincoln |
| EXTERMINATOR | Josh Stamberg |
| SHERRY | Judy Annozine |
| ORAL | James Stanley |
| CHUBBY BEF | Kate Gleason |
| DISTRICT MANAGER | Liam Craig |

It was later performed at HERE Arts Center in New York City. Change in cast:

| | |
|---|---|
| SHERRY | Chevon Rucker |
| DISTRICT MANAGER | Lakpa Bhutia |

# 1

*5:00 A.M. The restaurant is not open. Donald, the Restaurant Manager, appears. He is looking at small pieces of paper.*
*Exterminator taps on the window. Donald lets him in.*

EXTERMINATOR: Okay.
DONALD: Leave that door open.

# 2

*Oral, Sherry and Chubby Bef enter. Donald is talking to the group.*

DONALD: I want you to think about something for a minute . . .
Our food. The food we make . . . Want you to think about the
food we make in regards to the community. Think about
community for a minute—the people we serve—do you know?
You know. Bankers. Clergy. Teachers. Businessmen. You've
seen them—people who for the most part work hard. All
day. Think about the food we make and those people who
you know are eating it . . . I like to look at the big picture.

    The consumer—in the large sense nourished by us. By you
and by me. Our food going out, entering the community.

    I want you to think about yourself now. Think about how

hard you work . . . Mopping the floor, handling food, taking out the trash . . . And then you're done. You're done working. What do you want when you leave here? . . . You go into a store and what do you want . . . Do you want to stand in line? Do you want terrible service? Do you want dirty service?

Now think about our customers again. How hard these people work . . . They're no different than you. They want the same things that you do. What do they want? They want fast, clean, courteous service.

Now think about yourself again. Handling food, mopping the floor, taking out the trash . . . You can see yourself working now? I want you to be sanitary. I want you to be clean. You need to be clean. I want you to be courteous. I want you to be prompt.

. . . Our food going out into the community. Our food providing nourishment for the community.

## 3

*Workstations: employees go to work, e.g., drive-thru, cook and counter clerk, etc.*

## 4

*Donald is talking to the group.*

DONALD: A lot of customers have been complaining to me about our Whopper . . . I think a lot of what these reactions are to, uh, when the Whopper gets steamed because we haven't— we've made too many, during lunch and dinner rush. And they get re-heated in the microwave. And they're not broiler-fresh. This is a problem because we don't want people to think we're microwaving the meat and bun—because we're not—we are, but that's not what we want.

You all know the difference between steamed and flame-broiled . . .

The way to combat it is . . . make sure that we're on top of ordering—and not cooking more than we need to. Oral has been explaining to the customers that it is a state mandate that all burgers are microwaved, and although this is true, I would advise those of you to refrain from explaining this . . . Don't want to hear that. It's not important.

I think the thing to do is—if you know someone and they've, because they've complained before, or—ask them, "Would you like that off the broiler?" That way they know that you're concerned, and . . . they'll—believe me, they won't complain again.


# 5

*Workstations: Sherry and Oral. Oral is holding a small piece of paper.*

ORAL: 14. 14? . . . 14 . . . . . . . . . . . 14.


# 6

*Sherry is talking to Oral.*

SHERRY: I'm tired of her being lazy. She's lazy. You seen her. I'm doing more than my share of work. I'm sick of that. She's

always on the phone. She's on there all day. Customers are
waiting and she's on the phone.

ORAL: Who?

SHERRY: Bef. You know who I'm talking about. You seen her.

ORAL: Okay.

SHERRY: . . . I don't know. You know what to do. You seen her.
I'm just tired of it, that's all.

ORAL: All right, let me talk to her.

SHERRY: Thank you. Thank you, Oral.


# 7

*Donald is talking to the group.*

DONALD: Good morning and welcome to the 23rd meeting of the
Northeast Sector, Restaurant 6. I would like to note that
myself, Sherry, Oral and Chubby Bef are present. I, Donald,
am presiding . . . If you're working on something and you
stop and think about what you're working on . . . you screw
it up. I know. I've done this. So stop and think about that.
Don't—what do—what do you think we need to prevent this
from happening? . . . Well, I'll tell you. You need an activity
that will help your mind detach itself from your body. Chew
gum. Chew some gum. This will distract you enough.

BEF: We're not allowed to chew gum.

DONALD: Huh? Oh.

BEF: It says in the manual about it. We can't chew gum on the job.

DONALD: I know, I know. That manual may be out of date.

BEF: So why did you say it?

DONALD: What? No, nothing. I'm—

ORAL: Donald, we should get back to work. There are customers
waiting.

DONALD: Yes. By all means. Go back to work.

# 8

*Workstations:*

ORAL: Gimme a Chicken Snackrs! . . . And a Big Fish!
BEF: Order up!
ORAL: NO, I need Dino Snackrs!
BEF: You said Chicken Snackrs!!
SHERRY: Gimme a Chew-Chew Dino toy!
ORAL: I meant Dino Snackrs.
SHERRY: And I need an Eat, Eat A Lot!

# 9

*Sherry is talking to Oral.*

SHERRY: I'm thinking about going for Shift Coordinator. What do you think? Do you think I might be able to be Shift Coordinator.
ORAL: That's what I am. You want to be a Shift Coordinator?
SHERRY: Yeah.
ORAL: Okay. Have you ever worked at any other places that serve food?
SHERRY: No, this is my first.
ORAL: Okay. 'Cause it helps if you have other experience.
SHERRY: Did you?
ORAL: I worked at Flukey's.
SHERRY: What's that?
ORAL: Hot dog place.
SHERRY: Oh, wow. Okay. I just figure—
ORAL: You do a good job though. Maybe—
SHERRY: I figure, Donald seems to think I'm a good worker.

ORAL: Uh-huh. Have you memorized all that stuff in the manual?
SHERRY: Pretty much all of it. Maybe you could help me with—
ORAL: Oh, I don't think so. I don't really talk to him.
SHERRY: Not with Donald, though. I was hoping you could help
 me go through the stuff sometime.
ORAL: Oh. Yeah, okay.
SHERRY: Well, only if you want to.
ORAL: No, it's fine.
SHERRY: Thanks. I'd like that. I'd like that very much.

# 10

*Donald is talking to the group. He has the team handbook in his
hands.*

DONALD: I have something to say. I challenge you to challenge
 all that is written. Don't believe it simply because it is written down. I know that it all comes down to what is knowable. We say that something is knowable, what does that
 mean?—to know—and I used to think that I knew what it
 meant. It meant putting it into practice—take what has
 been put on paper or said to you and put it to the test . . .
 Grew to realize that there were just too many variables for
 me to count on experience. What worked for me once,
 wouldn't work on Thursday or Friday night. Wouldn't work
 when folks came in.
  But I want there to be something—after all my years that
 I know something. One thing. Anything. One truth . . . And if
 the only thing—the only thing that I know to be knowable is
 that nothing is knowable—at least then I have my one truth.

*Sings:*

> Bring me everyone
> The chain has begun
> Clean stainless steel
> I see it all
> Bring me everyone
> The chain has begun!
> Bring me everyone.

# 11

*Oral is talking to Sherry.*

ORAL: Hello, Sherry. I really like my job. Yeah. I think I'm pretty happy . . . For me, I'm sayin . . . I mean I think the best way for me to explain it is—how I feel would be to put it into these terms. I think the best way for me to put it—my happiness—is to put it into something . . . will be to put it in these terms. I feel happiness from the . . . motions I make, I feel—humbled by it . . . also get a lot out of it, the community my work with the team brings; there is pain, also, that reminds me of how important it is not to be selfish. I know how it is to have to get up at 4 in the morning, to come in and go in the freezer every day. But . . . I know why I do it. This way, I never lose touch with how much I can do. This keeps my relationship with my money good . . . I know what I'm worth, you know what I mean? . . . I'm just telling you about my job.
SHERRY: Wait. Did you get up at 4 or did you get to work at 4?

*Donald enters.*

DONALD: Did you see all of that?

ORAL: All of what?

DONALD: The delivery.

ORAL: Yeah. I put it all away.

DONALD: Oh. Thanks . . . Do you think you could come up front
and give me a hand?

ORAL: Sure.

*Donald and Oral exit.*
*Sherry sings:*

SHERRY:

    I like Oral
    Not the Manager
    But the Assistant Manager
    I like Oral
    Not the Manager
    But the Assistant Manager
    There is a certain something
    About him that I like
    About him that I like
    I like Oral.

*Bef enters.*

BEF: Oral? You like Oral? He's—works for the store.

SHERRY: What do you mean? What are we?

BEF: I don't know.

SHERRY: No, wait. What do you mean?

BEF: He wants to be here. We don't want to be here.

SHERRY: I know. He told me.

BEF: You like him though.

SHERRY: I don't know.

BEF: Yeah you do.

SHERRY: I don't know, man. What's that?

BEF: It's a letter.

SHERRY: Why? Are you sick?

BEF: No. For Donald. I want him to look at these things I wrote down about what could be better about this job.

SHERRY: Okay.

BEF: I'm asking all the people who work here to sign it. Can I get you to sign it?

SHERRY: "The Service Industry or the people in it don't know how much more they can take of it." *(Looks at Bef)* "Management has taken all the credit and money for the work that is done." What's that from?

BEF: What do you mean? It's true. This country depends on service. This is a service country. Imagine this country without fast foods, without dry cleaners or car washers? I'm going a ask everybody to leave this place if I don't get at least some of these things.

SHERRY: Ha ha. I can't.

BEF: I don't see what's so funny about that.

SHERRY: Where is there a place where someone can't always do our jobs for lower pay? Name one. They start at $5.15. You don't want to work for that? That's okay. We'll pay $4.75. And they will. And people will work for it. Mexicans or whatever.

BEF: No. Not since the minimum wage went up. It went up on September 1st.

SHERRY: You know what I mean. This company isn't that bad. You get benefits after a while.

BEF: But it has to—it's different than that. There's no job protection.

SHERRY: So what? So what are you going to do, Bef?

BEF: I told you. See? A letter with a list of demands. I'm a going a show it to Donald and then I'm going a show it to the District Manager.

SHERRY: Okay!

BEF: I want to know if you're going a sign your name on it.

## 1 2

*Workstations.*

## 1 3

*Donald is talking to the group.*

DONALD: As you are all—know, we're getting ready for the
arrival of the District Manager this week. You know this . . .
I want you to know that I'm very proud of all of you. I want
you to know that. I know in my heart that you are the team
that deserves to see the District Manager.

So, starting today, I want all of you to begin to look at
yourselves . . . Start looking at yourselves. And I'm not just
talking about your appearance: uniform, hair. I'm talking
about your inside. I want you to pay attention to that. I want
to know if you're feeling happy. I want to see that. I want
you to know that. The distance between what you look like
on the outside and what is going on inside, is, nothing. I'm
talking about your soul everybody. And I want to say forget
about the District Manager. Who cares. I don't care. For
right now, whatever. I want to think about my crew as beautiful people—completely . . . from the inside. Uniforms,
I don't care about that. I'll be truthful. Honestly, I don't care
what it says in the handbook. Grow your hair long, don't
shave your arm hair, stop brushing your teeth. I don't care.
I want my food handlers, my crew, to be happy. I want the
food they produce to be happy, and the people who eat will
be happy. Clean Community. Many making one. I love you
for that . . . I really do. Now go back to work.

*Donald exits.*

## 14

*Sherry, Bef and Oral.*

BEF: Oral. Don't listen to Sherry. She made up her mind about it.

SHERRY: We make minimum wage. Who cares about us? We're nobody. So, I'm saying what are you fighting for?

BEF: Now we make minimum wage. We don't have to make minimum wage—and that's not all. Oral, do you know that we could be fired at any time, without warning, without explanation, without a reason—it says right in the handbook about it.

ORAL: Who's this?

SHERRY: Is that right?

BEF: Yeah, what kind of protection is that? No security.

SHERRY: Yeah . . .

ORAL: No one's going to fire anybody.

SHERRY: That's right.

BEF: I'm serious. But what if we walked out, Sherry? Especially that the District Manager is coming. Donald won't want to disrupt anything right before he comes. Think about it. If we leave right before the District Manager comes in, he's going a hire all new people that he'll have to train. The store'll be shut down. He'll have to listen to us. Think about it. What's the District Manager going a think if he gets here and Donald is here all by himself.

SHERRY: You know what I think is funny, Oral? . . . Bef's the laziest person here. And the laziest person here wants to leave. Wants to stop working. I think that's funny.

ORAL: No.

BEF: Stop saying that!! I work harder than you!

SHERRY: How is that? I'd like a vacation myself.

ORAL: Sherry. Bef isn't lazy.

BEF: You don't care about any of us, you just want to use the work we do to help yourself.

ORAL: Time to relax . . .

SHERRY *(To Bef)*: No, it's not.

ORAL: Hey that's enough. No one's going to get fired.

*Bef goes back to work.*

SHERRY: So, what should I do?

ORAL: What about?

SHERRY: The District Manager.

ORAL: Oh, yeah.

SHERRY: Do you think I could talk to him?

ORAL: What for?

SHERRY: Well, you know. I'd like to run this store. I'd like to. And
    I can.

ORAL: I know.

SHERRY: What?

ORAL: No. I don't—

SHERRY: You think what?

ORAL: I don't know if you're . . .

SHERRY: Why not?

ORAL: No. You should talk to him.

SHERRY: I'm going to talk to him.

ORAL: Okay.


# 15

*The District Manager. Everyone is present.*

DISTRICT MANAGER: Yes. Hello everyone. Thank you for wel-
    coming me into your store. I've heard many good things
    about the Northeast Region and this store in particular . . .
    Yes, I know I've heard your name Donald mentioned favor-
    ably a number of times. I'm looking forward to these next

couple of hours. I'm looking forward to getting to know all of you. After all, I started in this as a food handler myself. Yes.

I'd like to start today with a get-to-know-you quiz. This quiz is a chance for us to find out who each of us is. Okay? I want to find out. Okay. Here's pencils . . . A lot of pencils! Ready? Yes. First question—Out of all the fast-food restaurants you can think of, who has the best-tasting hamburgers: McDonald's, Wendy's, Hardees or Burger King? . . . Okay? Everybody ready? Yes. Next. Which fast-food chain has the best burger value for the money: McDonald's, Wendy's, Hardees or Burger King? . . . Okay? Yes. Next. Choose from the following—in your opinion, if you could work at any fast-food restaurant, which would you choose: Sloppy Jo's, Taco Bell, George Washington's or Burger King? Okay. Good. Yes. Finally. Which of the following perks do you have during a 6-hour shift: a 10-minute break, a synchronized-watch period, or all the soda you can drink? . . . Okay? Good. Yes. Go ahead and turn those in . . . Let me see them . . .

*The District Manager looks at their answers.*

DONALD: . . . Of course we're pleased that the District Manager is here . . .

As you can see, we have a lot of things to offer you . . . ah . . . a lot of things. We got . . . the free drinks. Ah, we got— right? You get free drinks whenever you want, right? I assume you knew that. Yeah . . . you do. But I'm sure you knew that! . . . I'm thinking about some changes here anyway. I don't like the interior . . . Never did. I—don't you think, hey— don't you think some plants would look nice in this atrium area? I do. Mister. Hey. What about some money for the plants?

DISTRICT MANAGER:

DONALD: . . . I would like to see some changes, yeah . . . Yeah! How much money do you have for that kind of thing? . . .

Mister. Hey. Paint. Plants. Re-pave it. The parking lot . . .
Everything. Yeah, do it. DO IT . . . Yeah. It's not a bad thing.
Yeah! District Manager. I'm just not convinced that it's just
not anything. It's nothing. I, it's not, I wanna—I wanna—
I wanna—!!!!!

DISTRICT MANAGER:

*Donald exits followed by the District Manager.*


# 1 6

*Workstations: Donald is talking to the group.*

DONALD: Hey, everybody. I just remembered something. When
I was your age, I worked at Paradise Burger. I was working
by myself. In those days, food handlers would just decide
not to show up for work. Not like today. Anyway, I had a few
days like this where it had been ages since a customer had
come in and I had been by myself for a long time—in fact,
I was reading a magazine. When in walks this man wearing
a suit on a Saturday. I really wanted to go home. I was angry
at him for coming in. He placed his order. He wanted the
Special we were having—something that nobody was buying. I had to go into the walk-in cooler to get the special
patty. I was looking for the meat and I finally found it buried
under some boxes. When I brought it out and put it on the
grill, I noticed the meat had turned a pale brown. I looked
up to see the man watching me. He was looking at me. But
he didn't notice the rotten meat. I knew it was rotten, and
for some reason I couldn't take the meat off the grill. It
seemed too much of a hassle to take the time to explain that
the meat had gone bad and would you like something else?
Because I didn't want him to notice the mistake. I didn't

want him to notice that our store made a mistake. So I decided to serve him the meat. Now I think about it, I actually did this a number of times—to save myself from embarrassment.

*Oral sings:*

ORAL:
Hello.
Can you feel the love tonight?
Can you feel the love tonight?
Tonight?

Hello.
Can you hear HVAC?
Can you hear HVAC?
Tonight?

Hello.
Can you see the great bright white?
I can see the great bright white.
Tonight.

# 17

*5:00 A.M. The restaurant is not open. Oral, the Restaurant Manager, appears. He is looking at small pieces of paper.*
  *Exterminator taps on the window. Oral lets him in.*

EXTERMINATOR: Okay.
ORAL: Leave that door open.
EXTERMINATOR: Where's that short dude?
ORAL: What?

# UTE MNOS V. CRAZY LIQUORS

*Ute Mnos v. Crazy Liquors* premiered in February 1998 at Eden Arcade in New York City. Direction by the author. Set and lights by Eric Dyer. Costumes by Sibyl Kempson. Original cast:

| | |
|---|---|
| BAILIFF/DARYL | Ryan Bronz |
| KIM GEEVER | Emily Cass McDonnell |
| JUDGE | Bob Feldman |
| JOE | Yehuda Duenyas |
| PROSECUTING ATTORNEY/MIKE | Lakpa Bhutia |
| TERRY | Jaymes Brevard |
| RANDALL | Gary Wilmes |
| CRAZY | Jack Doulin |
| SOAPY | Ford Wright |
| UTE MNOS | Kevin Hurley |

Band:

Andrew Bergman (Bass)
Nicholas French (Guitar)
Christopher Kirkman (Guitar)
Jamie Montgomery (Drums)

# ACT 1

## 1          KIM GEEVER

*The courtroom. A deadbolt turns. Bailiff, Kim Geever, Judge and Joe enter.*

BAILIFF: Ah . . . Kim Geever, Terry Wright, Randall Eilif and Crazy.

KIM: This is Kim Geever . . . I remember him trying to serve himself behind the bar. We've had him in Crazy's. He was in there a lot—

JOE: Wait, wait, wait—

JUDGE: Objection!

JOE: Whoa—Objection?! I haven't said anything, Judge . . . What is happening?

JUDGE: Okay . . . It's okay. She can talk. *(To Kim)* Go ahead.

KIM: . . . I remember him trying to serve himself behind the bar. We've had him in Crazy's. He was in there a lot. I think he lived around there. And I don't know if he was—he seemed pretty drunk. I've seen him drunk before. He was pretty drunk. But I never knew him to be rowdy or—not rowdy 'cause he did get rowdy, Ute did, but, he was never dangerous. I never thought he was dangerous. Let's put it that way. Drunk but not dangerous. He wasn't dangerous. I never thought he was dangerous. But Mike was behind the bar

73

and went over and talked to him. I didn't hear what he said. It was loud. I think he might have, there might have been a problem with one of the football players. There was a problem. —There was this girl who was at the bar—a man was standing behind. And there was a man behind her. He looked like he was with her. And then Ute behind him. And I looked away for a second, or I went to do something and I heard a sound, and I looked up and there was that girl at the bar and she hit her head. And somehow they had switched positions. And the girl was holding her head. She hit her head. Mike came from behind the bar and went out and took Ute to where I couldn't see him. I went back to whatever I was doing. And then later Randall went out, and then came back and said that I should go outside and see Ute . . . Um . . . So I went outside to check on Ute. I asked him, if he had a place to go, to stay. I know he was kicked out of the one place he was living at—did he have a place to stay? He said, "Yes." I said, "Why don't you go over there?" He said because his leg was broken. Broken. I said, "Which one?" He said, "This one!" And he just kinda slapped his leg like it was no big deal, and I said, "Are you sure?" He said, "Yeah! It's broken!" So I came back in and I said I don't know if his leg is—broken. I think he'd be in more pain if his leg was broken. But he said his leg was broken. His leg was broken . . . Sometimes when they get really drunk, they can't, they don't feel the pain. You know one time we had a guy who had his throat slashed in there, and didn't even know it was slashed, he was so drunk.

JOE: Great. It's a Saturday night?

*Door buzzer sounds, Bailiff speaks into intercom.*

BAILIFF: Yeah.
VOICE: Isthihfthis. Ygqt. Thyw zhdr sssss . . . ?

*Bailiff presses button.*

KIM: Yeah, it was right after a football game and 5-dollar pitchers, so we get a lot of people.

JOE: Was Randall working that night?

KIM: No.

JOE: Great. Terry was a bouncer?

KIM: Yes.

JOE: Okay. What kind of opinion do you have of him?

KIM: Of Terry?

JOE: Yeah.

KIM: As far as I know, he seems nice. I think he's nice.

JOE: He's been in the bar before?

KIM: He came in there quite a bit.

JOE: Has he ever gotten drunk in there?

KIM: No.

JOE: Have you ever seen him obnoxious?

KIM: Ah, no, I saw him—punch somebody once.

JOE: Do you have any idea what for?

KIM: He got called a racial name.

JOE: Okay. Do you know from the times that you've seen him and I realize you haven't spent that much time with him is he slow to anger or quick to anger?

KIM: He seems mellow. Or nice. That's why I was really surprised—

JOE: Would you say that about Randall Eilif too?

KIM: No. I think Randall has got a quick temper . . . especially when he gets drunk.

JOE: Was he drunk that night?

KIM: I would assume so. Yeah. I don't really know.

JOE: Great. Do you think he had anything to do with Ute's condition?

KIM:

JOE: Instead of Terry.

KIM: That's a tough question . . .

JOE: You're thinking about it. There must be a reason.

JUDGE: That's a good question.

KIM *(To Joe)*: Yeah. Him and Terry are very good friends. So, he may have decided to do Terry's job, because he's standing up for Terry, instead of Terry doing it. I wouldn't put it past me if Randall was the one who hurt Ute, and not Terry . . . What does Ute say?

JOE: He doesn't know. He's a total blackout. Total blackout. We're trying to put the night back together.

*Buzzer.*

JUDGE: Ute?

*Kim exits.*

BAILIFF: I think that's Terry.

*There is a an attempt to open the door from the outside. The Bailiff grabs his keys and opens the lock.*

## 2                                    TERRY WRIGHT

*Prosecuting Attorney (P.A.) enters.*

JOE: Can I help you?

P.A.: YEAH, UH, I—HOW YOU DOIN. THEY SAID I COULD COME DOWN AND TRAIL YOU GUYS. IS THAT COOL?

JOE: You're with us?

P.A.: YEAH. I'M TRYING TO BE PROSECUTING—I *WAS* PROSECUTING, THEN I CAME OVER HERE.

JOE: Who sent you down here?

P.A.: THE GUY—THE AH—THE GUY—AH! WHAT'S HIS NAME. RAH!—I CAN'T THINK OF IT. I HAVE—HE GAVE A NUMBER TO CALL . . . DO YOU WANT TO CALL HIM?

JOE: No. Okay. I guess have a seat. You're going to trail us?

P.A.: YES.

JOE: Okay.

*Another knock. Terry Wright enters.*

BAILIFF: Do you swear you're gonna give the truth?

TERRY: I do.

JOE: . . . Go.

TERRY: . . . Okay, he came in and uh, the back door where I was
    working, which I thought was the front because they come
    in the front, but it was the back, and, he was—

JOE: Who he? He who?

TERRY: The guy.

JOE: Ute?

TERRY: Whatever his name is. I can't pronounce it.

JOE: Okay. Ute is. Go ahead . . .

TERRY: I don't know if he was—I couldn't tell if he was really
    drunk, at first, but he came in and I charged him proper
    charge for money and ID, and he said he was only gonna go
    in buy beer, so I didn't charge him. I let him in so he could
    come up, and I saw him sit down so right there he lied to
    me. But I figured, I kind of just let it slide, and then, I don't
    know if it was an hour or 2 hours, whatever, the guys rushed
    him out—he had—apparently he had done something,
    I didn't see, you know, but they rushed him out of the door.
    Stinko, and Sully. They took him out. And then he came
    back in and—I told him he couldn't come in, because they
    threw him out—apparently he'd done something wrong,
    and he insisted on going back in, I said no, and um, he
    grabbed my jacket, like, the jacket that I had on—and I just
    laughed it off, 'cause I'm not a violent person. But I am from
    a different area. I just, he grabbed my jacket and I put his
    hands down and I told him he had to leave. And he insisted
    on going back in. I, he was, he was drunk, I could tell he was
    drunk. You know, he grabbed my jacket again and I took his

hands down and I said to him, "Get out." And he said, "I'm going back in." So he had to be drunk to grab me 3 times. And I kinda shoved him in the face. He fell down and I said Randall get him out because I was mad. And I said get him out of here and I just didn't want to be bothered with him no more. And they took him, Randall took him out and that was it. I was—I wasn't really afraid of him. —Well, I was afraid of what could happen, you know just instincts, you know, from the way I was brought up, you know, it's a whole different situation. You don't give a guy 3 chances. I mean, I'm not saying this to be on the record or anything. I'm just saying the way I was raised, you know, and so it was kind of instincts and for him to grab my jacket and me to shove him 'cause I don't usually just go around shoving people. I was really trying to get distance—put it like that. I wasn't afraid of him but anything could happen.

JOE: Do you think he might have had a weapon?

TERRY: He may have, he may have, I don't know.

JOE: Were you afraid of that?

TERRY: It crossed my mind. For him to grab my jacket and then me be 6' 2" 300 pounds, you know, someone's either, you're drunk, crazy, or got a weapon.

JOE: Did you hit Ute?

TERRY: Push. It wasn't a hit. Not a closed fist hit, no.

JOE: Think it was hard enough to break his jaw?

TERRY: I wasn't trying to decapitate the guy, or, 'cause, I mean, you look at the two, and if I was trying to really hurt him, I could've hurt him. But, I wasn't trying to hurt him. I was trying to get, you know, room.

JOE: Did you talk to Crazy that next day?

TERRY: He talked to me.

JOE: Did he tell you then about your job there?

TERRY: Well, am I working there now?

JOE: Did he at that time, tell you anything about your future at Crazy's?

TERRY: Well, I . . .

JOE: What'd he say.

TERRY: Exact words?

JOE: As close as you can remember.

TERRY: Uh, you're through. At Crazy's.

JOE: He say why?

TERRY: No.

JOE: You didn't ask him why?

TERRY: No, I just took for granted it was because of the incident.

JOE: Great. Do you remember what you said to our P.I.?

TERRY: Not really . . .

JOE: I'd like to show this exhibit. Exhibit 1.


*Joe hands Terry a piece of paper.*
  *Buzzer.*


Do you recall now?

TERRY: Yep.

JOE: And this statement was taken October 31st.

TERRY: I guess that's exact. You should know . . .

JOE: You would trust this more than that? Or that more than this.

TERRY: Not really, I mean, if I said something today that I didn't say there, then I could correct the two.

JOE: Where are you from?

TERRY: Baton Rouge, Louisiana.

JOE: When did you first come up here?

TERRY: Ah . . . last year . . . of May May 18, 19, something like that.

JOE: So, you've been here about a year . . .

TERRY: Umm-hmm . . . But I've been going back and forth.

JOE: Have you had any jobs since you came up here?

TERRY: I worked at Crazy's.

JOE: Have you had any other, employment?

TERRY: No.

JOE: When did you begin working at Crazy's?

TERRY: I can't remember, man, exactly . . . I can't remember.

JOE: Would September 23. Would you disagree with that?

TERRY: I can't agree 'cause I don't know, but, probably around that time. Probably. You should know . . . It's your case.

P.A. *(To Terry)*: HEY . . .

JOE: You have no reason to doubt me.

TERRY: Right.

JOE: And for how long did you work there?

TERRY: 1 night.

JOE: How did you get the job there at Crazy's?

TERRY: Umm, well . . . I knew Crazy. And some of the players football players and one of my close friends, closest friends that I have up here, he works there. Randall Eilif. And uh, he started, hooked me up with the job.

JOE: Did you fill out an application?

TERRY: No.

JOE: Did you receive any instructions on your duties?

TERRY: No, mean, it's simple, I mean, doorman, simple.

JOE: But Crazy never sat down with you and told you these were your job duties, your—

TERRY: No.

JOE: Did you fill out a W—

TERRY: 2 form? No.

JOE: Did you get paid for the night that you worked?

TERRY: I did.

JOE: Have you been arrested for assault?

TERRY: Never.

JOE: How about before this incident, you were in Crazy's bar. Is that correct?

TERRY: Yeah, probably, yeah.

JOE: Do you know a friend of Ute's named Soapy?

TERRY: Oh, yeah, I know what you're talking about. I know exactly what you're talking about.

JOE: What is that?

TERRY: Ah, you gonna ax me did we get into an incident?

JOE: What, what happened there?

TERRY: I was there, uh, it was Thursday. Or maybe it might've been after one of the games. And, um the guy came up . . .

JOE: Who is that?

TERRY: The guy that you're talking about.

JOE: Soapy?

TERRY: Right.

JOE: You—

TERRY: He came up and he was talking to me and we were talking nice. I guess he went off and got a little tipsy. Came back over and he axed me, "How does it feel to be a nigger in a white man's world?" And I said, you know, it kind of shocked me, but, I axed I said, "What did you say?" You know, and he said it again, and I said well could you define that word and he said you know what I'm talking about—black, blacks always be that to him. And out of rage, maybe just temper, we got into it.

JOE: Did you hit him?

TERRY: Yeah.

JOE: Where?

TERRY: I don't know. Somewhere. Once.

JOE: Somewhere?

TERRY: Right. And then I left.

JOE: And then you left?

TERRY: Right.

JOE: When you were with, with Ute in the back did he say any racist remark to you?

TERRY: Ah, no. Before that he called me "Buck-Buck." But I never knew what a "Buck-Buck" was so I paid no mind.

JOE: Did you have anything to drink that night?

TERRY: No.

JOE: I'm talking about the September 23rd incident . . .

TERRY: Did I ever . . . ?

JOE: Incident.

TERRY: No.

JOE: . . . Okay. I guess no more questions. Thank you.

JUDGE: I don't have any questions.

JOE *(To P.A.)*: Do you want to—?
P.A.: UH, YEAH . . . DID YOU HURT YOUR HAND WHEN YOU
    HIT UTE?
TERRY: No.
JOE: . . . That's it?

*Terry exits.*

You can ask more questions.
P.A.: NO. THAT'S IT.


3                                      RANDALL EILIF

*Randall Eilif enters.*

BAILIFF: Randall Eilif . . .
RANDALL: . . . This is Randall, Randall P. Eilif . . . Ute said some-
    thing to Terry and he pushed Terry and you know, kinda
    made Terry feel insecure I suppose. And Terry hit him. And,
    well, being the fact that he's not from here, and he's ah, they
    have different values, different norms, and he when Ute was
    doin, you know pressing him like that, and ah, Terry's been
    shot at and everything by skinnier people and so that's, he's
    been a bouncer before, so I'm sure you know, he'd know,
    you know, certain things and he just felt insecure is the way
    I saw 'cause he was, Ute was grabbin you know, and Terry
    said no and pushed him away and then he grabbed him
    again. And I know from workin that, you don't—I don', well,
    Crazy's son, Jeff said not to use . . . too much force would
    be . . . 'cause they gave me an example, basically, what hap-
    pened on the east side where some guy got thrown through
    the window and they didn't want that to happen to, you
    know . . . That's what. So they basically said, you know, let

them strike first before you strike them. Not that way, but, you know the interpretation that I took it was. An' as far as gettin people out—to remove them, they said just remove em out of the way. I mean, you had to get them out of there. Not by . . . I don't know how to ex—I mean, ah, I mean there wadn't anything about taking em out by force or anything like that. I mean, ah, if someone's gonna try to give you trouble to get em out, you have to use whatever way you can get them out of there. If they're going to give you resistance, you gotta give a little more to get em out, but, you know, more, tryin to cooperate between 2 people than doin actual physical damage.

JOE: Okay, have you done this before?

RANDALL: What—

JOE: This. You know your responses have to be verbal.

RANDALL: Yes.

JOE: We can't take a nod of the head.

RANDALL: Yes.

JOE: A gesture, so . . .

RANDALL: . . . Yes.

JOE: Where do you live?

RANDALL: Okay, I'm at Joseph House—#65 South Avenue, apartment 18. That's Sline—Sline Hall.

JOE: Phone number?

RANDALL: Ah, 33—3326—332-346.

JOE: . . . I have . . .

RANDALL: Okay, it's 3—332-6346.

JUDGE: This guy has trouble speaking.

JOE: How old are you?

RANDALL: Ah, 23.

JOE: Do you play sports?

RANDALL: I was—I was involved in football, outside linebacker, but this year—this is my senior year, so I've been put on— the ineligibility list.

JOE: What do you study?

RANDALL: Ah, physical education.

JOE: Do you anticipate to graduate?

RANDALL: Yes. Yes. I'm going to. Corporate fitness.

JOE: Okay. And what is your height and weight?

RANDALL: 6 foot. 320.

JOE: Did you see Terry hit Ute?

RANDALL: Yes, I did. I seen him.

JOE: Where did he hit him?

RANDALL: In, in the, ah, face.

JOE: How did he hit him?

RANDALL: Swung at him, I don't know how to really explain it, just swung with his right arm.

JOE: With a fist?

RANDALL: Yes.

JOE: Closed fist?

RANDALL: Yes.

JOE: Tell me what happened after Ute was hit.

RANDALL: He was hit, and I took him outside and laid him up against ah, against the sidewalk. There's right on the south side of the wall, right next to ah, there's a meter right there. A water meter. And ah, set him there. I set him there and I really didn't want him to swallow his tongue you know I was—and then he started coming to . . . and Kim just came out, you know Kim came out there and we kinda sat there and talked about what happened inside and everything. And then, we, ah, went back inside. For about 20 or 30 minutes and then I came back outside. And he was tryin to come back in again.

JOE: . . . The first time you took him out you set him around the corner you, you and Ute both went out the door and you set him around the corner of the building, by the meter?

RANDALL: Yes.

JOE: And then you went back into the bar?

RANDALL: No, no. I was stay—I set out there.

JOE: You sat out there.

RANDALL: Yes.

JOE: For how long?

RANDALL: Probably about 15 minutes. Till he came to . . . then, well, between that time, Kim came outside and within that time, he woke up, and he was speaking gibberish. He wasn't really saying anythin clear or anything. And then we just kinda talked and then went back inside. And then I went back outside, later, probably 15 minutes and he was, he came over and tried to come back in, and I more or less told, you, you can't come back in here. You know they'd already thrown you out and, look what happened to you. And so I just, more or less, redirected him 'cause I thought he lived upstairs. So I redirected him to the north. Being that the ah, way to get upstairs is through the front north door. And so I redirected there, just kinda patted him whatever and redirected him and he just went down. There really wadn't no physical, I mean this, there's no way—I pushed people and everything so I know how much force I can exert to a person and the force that I put on him was not even nowhere near that, you know, could be exerted and he fell down right there . . . And he lay there and I said well you gotta go, he said, he said I'm not going anywhere, you know, and so, basically he said I can't move. So I said okay. So I went back inside. I didn't help him because he was, when he was sayin that he was smilin and laughin, and so I didn't you know know if he was, just the alcohol was doin it or he just, or what. So I just went back inside.

JOE: Did you have anything to drink that night?

RANDALL: Yes. I wadn't working, so, you know I went there, intending, you know, to have a good time.

JOE: What were you drinking?

RANDALL: Just beer. Straight beer.

JOE: You didn't have any mixed drinks that night?

RANDALL: No . . . well, I, maybe I may a had ah, a straight shot. You know, but I didn't have more than maybe 1 or 2, that's, but I had a couple pitchers. Well, I really couldn't tell you 'cause I . . . probably about 2 or 3 pitchers, couple shots, and they were, when I mean shots, I don't mean straight shots of ah, it was more of an Amaretto Slammer, it was Amaretto and then there's Seven-Up on top of it . . . I didn't drink 2 or 3 pitchers. I drank with David in the back bar with 2 and 3 pitchers with his girlfriend. We were just talkin old times. Stuff like that. I wad going back from talkin to him to going up front to talk to Terry at the door.

JOE: They have any drink specials on that night?

RANDALL: 5-dollar pitchers.

JOE: The 3 of you drank 2 or 3 pitchers.

RANDALL: Yes. Medium pitcher specials.

JOE: Who's David?

RANDALL: Tight end from Michigan . . . *(To Judge)* You know, they're like those pitchers—I don't know how you explain. I wonder if you've ever—at TGIF Friday's. Those pitchers aren't very big. Or like Bennigans. You know. No, brah. Is like Houlihans. They have those. That's what.

JOE: Did you strike Ute at all?

RANDALL: No. Never struck him . . . I had no, I had no reason to strike him. He was, he was too drunk already, and there was no reason to. He was, you know, bleeding, and everything else.

JOE: Where was he bleeding?

RANDALL: Just, ah, basically out the nose and mouth that I saw. Next thing, you know he's blabbering and there's no reason to do anything to him.

JOE: Do you know Ute to be a violent person?

RANDALL: No, I never know Ute to be a violent person.

JOE: Ever know him to carry a weapon?

RANDALL: Not that I know, but, you know violent people, when I say people I mean transients, who stay upstairs there, low income, they do a lot of things, to, to survive, you know, so I really didn't, I mean I didn't know him personally, but I'd known him from the bars scene, and most of the time I'd seen him, I'd never seen him sober.

JOE: You didn't perceive him as a threat that night?

RANDALL: No, that's why I went out there, you know, 'cause I wouldn't a went out there to see what he was doin if I really thought that, you know, if I didn't like him, if I had some kind ah, a vendetta against him or something.

JOE: I guess I have no more questions. *(To P.A.)* Do you want to ask questions?

P.A.: YES I HAVE A FEW QUESTIONS. AS I—UHH . . . I'LL JUST GO TO THE POINT WHERE—TERRY, HAD ACCORDING TO YOU—STRUCK, AH UTE. AND UTE COLLAPSED, KNEES GAVE WAY AND HE WAS ON THE FLOOR, BLEEDING—AND I UNDERSTAND YOU DRAGGED HIM?

RANDALL: I picked him up and just took him out, with both hands behind him, I just kinda pulled him up and set him up against the wall.

P.A.: YOU PULLED HIM OUT. HIS FACE WOULD BE UP, THE BACK OF HIS HEAD TOWARD THE FLOOR?

RANDALL: No, being that when I pulled him, he was, yes, his face was facing away.

P.A.: WOULD HIS HEELS HAVE BEEN DRAGGING?

RANDALL: Yes.

P.A.: WHEN YOU PULLED HIM OUT, HIS HEELS WERE DRAGGING RATHER THAN—

RANDALL: Yes, no his face when I, I mean I didn't pick him up, I didn't drag him out like a sack a potatoes, or anything like that.

P.A.: NO. I KNOW. WOULD THIS BE DRAGGING?

RANDALL: Well . . .

P.A.: OKAY.

JOE: All done? Okay.

*Randall exits.*

Ahh. I was up at 5 o'clock this morning. I had to take the bus . . . How long you been here?

JUDGE: . . . Like 6 months. 7 months.

P.A.: WHO'S THE NEXT GUY?

JOE: It's like, you're tired of questions, right?

JUDGE: Yeah . . . How long for you?

JOE: 12 months. 1 year.

JUDGE: Okay.

*They look at P.A.*

P.A.: WHAT?

JOE: Nothing . . . Did you just start?

P.A.: YEAH. I WAS WITH ANOTHER COMPANY BEFORE THIS.

JOE: Okay . . . It's Crazy. Crazy is next. Right, Judge?

JUDGE:

BAILIFF: Yeah.

JOE: I wonder how long he'll go?

JUDGE: Yeah.

*Buzzer.*

JUDGE: You woke up at 5? I—okay . . .

# 4                                        CRAZY

*Crazy enters.*

BAILIFF: Do you promise to tell the whole truth?

CRAZY: Yesssssssssssssssss . . .

JOE: Tell us your position and title at Crazy's.

CRAZY: . . . Pfhhh . . . Well, do you know my name?

JOE: Yes.

CRAZY: . . . And do you know the name of the bar?

JOE: Crazy—

CRAZY: Ha. Can you figure it out?

JOE: Crazy, this is for the record.

JUDGE: This is the 2nd time with this guy.

JOE: Mr. Crazy . . . We need your—your assistance . . .

CRAZY: Don't do me any favors. Who's doing who a favor? Let me straighten you out. I'm a businessman. Do you know the word "busy"? It comes from "business." I'm taking time out of my busy schedule so you can play around? You're playing. Playing around. Think about that. Lawyer: let me ask you a question. Before you ask me a question, think about the question. Make sure it's the right question, because— I'm not a—I'm not a jerk. I don't have time to get jerked— please don't jerk me around. Now. Judge!

JUDGE:

JOE: Mr. Crazy . . . okay. Can I remind you that you agreed to come here and you're here because of a lawsuit. This case has your name on it. This is an opportunity for you to present yourself as—to speak on your behalf, to tell your side of things. This—this is not supposed to, to malign anyone.

CRAZY: I *know*! It's like break out the peace pipe, right? This was a courtesy call. I have work to do. I have a basement full of filing cabinets. Full of papers, full of files. The filing cabinets are covered in dust. And those papers have turned yellow. We're on the computers. We don't need rusty filing cabinets in the basement. The numbers are on the receipts in the cabinets in the basement. Waiting for me to put on the computer. Numbers. Rusty filing cabinets. Pieces and pieces of paper. I do that. So. Will you please do your job so I can do mine? . . . I'm talking about the job I do.

*Crazy exits.*

JUDGE: Mr. Crazy is very busy.

JOE: Right?

BAILIFF: That's it?

JOE: Yeah.

*All exit.*

# ACT 2

THE BAR

*Time: September 23rd. Crazy Liquors. Loud. Crazy is giving instructions to Terry and Randall. Kim Geever, Mike and Daryl look on.*

CRAZY: Different types of people. Different groups. And they don't all get along. Civil servants, professionals, military, civilians, entrepreneurs. Blue collar, white collar. That's why there's so many fights. A lot of fights. Groups know what they will do. You can't be too careful. Remove like this and carefully you don't hurt the people. I give you so many examples of what can happen at this bar when things go wrong. I have a list of things not to do. It's called a list of don'ts. Above all else, I don't want any trouble in this place. Don't be the first to strike. Let them take the first swing. You were hired because I know you can take whatever they give. Don't worry. Who's going to mess with you. Look at your shoulders. That's hard work. You hit somebody. They're not getting up. A man would be stupid to mess with you. You can throw. And kick, too. Good . . . What time is it?

*Crazy exits. Music. Soapy enters, then Ute.*

UTE: Hi, Soapy. How are you!

SOAPY: Ha ha!

*They wrestle.*

　　Ess oh see kay ess?
UTE: Yeh! He's comin in. Dhet guy.
SOAPY: Aight. Aye like det, min. Ha!
UTE: Yeh. What's this dude's name?
SOAPY: Hoo ils?
UTE: What this—
SOAPY: Uh . . .
UTE: Look . . . *(Points at Kim)*
SOAPY: Haa!
UTE: Did he tell you bout det one dude?
SOAPY: Pehfe! Dhet yoo. Dhet yoo, doo! Ha ha!

*They wrestle again. Kim serves them drinks.*

KIM: All right!

*They pay.*

SOAPY: Hoo did et?
UTE: Yehh! . . .
SOAPY: Hoo?
UTE:

*He smiles.*

SOAPY: Shee wuz?
UTE: Yeh! . . .

*Terry enters.*

UTE: . . . Hey! Buck-Buck!
SOAPY: I like dis doo! Ha!

TERRY: All right . . .

UTE: Sit down.

TERRY: Thanks.

SOAPY: Yoo play footebahl?

TERRY: Right.

SOAPY: Me too, ha ha. Arrr!

TERRY: (Heh.)

UTE: You workin tonite?

TERRY: Later on, yeah.

SOAPY: Coool! . . . *(To Ute)* Jew hear? . . .

UTE: Huh?

SOAPY: Thet doo came a dtet—ive.

UTE: Who?

SOAPY: Yeah!

UTE: He did?

SOAPY: Now you're, "Les go My-imy!" right!?

UTE: He wouldn say that.

SOAPY: Wut?

UTE: Heed be: "I'm still de same, I haven change." You know: "I still me and you still you . . ." But is like, I say: "Does det mean you still gonna look de other way?" *(Screams)* When I break de law? Ha haa!!!!! Haa!!

SOAPY: Haaaaaah Ha!!! *(Wheezing)*

*Terry leaves.*

UTE: All right, Buck-Buck.

*Soapy smiles at Ute.*

. . . But do you know what he said? He said that that what he meant all along. Det he meant it! That why he said it . . . You believe that?

*Soapy is struck dumb by this. Terry returns with a beer.*

Hey, what took you so long.

SOAPY: Yeh wut tok yoo so lon . . . Hey! Lemme ax yoo . . . howse
    it feel to be a nigge inna white mins wirl?
TERRY: Excuse me?
UTE: Ehh. He's jus jokin.
SOAPY: Howse it feel to be a nigge inna white mins wirl?
TERRY: . . . Tell me what you mean by that word?
SOAPY: You know . . . black. Blacks. Das whut it mean to me.
    Always.
TERRY: You should watch your mouth if you don't have any-
    thing—
SOAPY: Wha?! Wha?!! Inna tyme—
TERRY: Garbage . . .
UTE: Duuude!!

*Terry hits Soapy.*

SOAPY: Ahh.

*Terry exits.*

UTE *(To Soapy)*: Hey . . .

*Kim sings:*

KIM:
            In times like these
            I always think of my father
            He told me always
            Turn the other cheek
            Jesus said to turn the other cheek, too
            In times like these I think of my father
            Turn the other cheek until you run out of cheeks
            When you run out of cheeks, Cheeky, start swinging
            And don't stop until there's no one left
            In times like these
            I think of my father.

*Ute enters.*

UTE: Hey Buck-Buck.
TERRY: Whoa. Where you going?
UTE: . . . Inside, no I ain' gonna—I'm jus gonna drink, dude.
TERRY: . . . All right . . . stay at the bar . . .

*Ute goes to the bar then walks over to the band area and sits
down with Soapy. Terry looks on.*

UTE: Hi, how are you.

*They wrestle.*

Where de ban?
SOAPY: Hoo?
UTE: Mu-sic!! Mu-sic!! Mu-sic!!
SOAPY *(With Ute)*: Mu-sit!! Mu-sit!! Ha haa. Hey, doo, geh *me* a
   drink.
UTE: Ahh.

*Randall passes.*

SOAPY: Thas guys uge. DES GUYS AR UGE! ALL DES GUYS AR
   UGE!!
UTE: Yeah . . .
SOAPY: Ey, geh *me* a *drink*!!
UTE: . . . Where's your money? Ahh.

*Ute goes to the bar.
   Terry sings:*

TERRY:
       Where has the love gone
       In this place
       Do you know?

Where has the love gone, do you know
Do you hear music, man
Don't it make you wanna get up and dance
I had a dream last night about my love
Not my new love or my now love
I'm saying my old love
My past love
And now I want to quit my now love
And call up my old love
And make her my new love.

*Ute at the bar talking to Kim. Randall is standing next to Ute talking to someone else.*

UTE: How you doin?
KIM: Fine.
UTE: Gimme some of that . . . You got no ass, Kimmy! Ha ha.
KIM: Okay. Stop it.
UTE: C'mon! I know you know you like me.
KIM: Oh, Ute. I do. You know I do. Deeply. Just not in that way.
UTE: Meanwhile . . . Is this your boyfriend?
KIM: No. Yes . . . Not really. Why? Will you be my boyfriend, Ute?
*(Laughs)*

*Ute pushes Randall from behind.*

RANDALL: Hey! *(Turns)*
UTE: Sorry.
RANDALL: Watch it. Hey. Don't fuckin spill my beer!
UTE: My fault.

*Randall turns back around. Ute smiles at Kim.*

That's your boyfriend!

*Ute pushes Randall.*

RANDALL: That's it! What the fuck—

UTE: Sorry. Sorry. Accident. Buy you a beer?

RANDALL: Somethin, little man. Somethin.

UTE: Sure. What's your name?

RANDALL: Why? What's yours?

UTE: Ute! An' you are?

RANDALL: Randall.

UTE: All right, Randall, let me tell you something. She likes you, dude.

RANDALL: Who?

UTE:

RANDALL: . . . That's my girlfriend. What the fuck is your problem? *(Grabs Ute)*

UTE: No no no! Come on. I gotta go to church tomorrow. C'mon. Let me buy you a drink.

RANDALL: I don't see a drink.

UTE: It's too damn busy.

RANDALL: Little man, you're walking on thin glass.

KIM *(To Ute)*: You're a freak.

UTE *(In her ear)*: I love you. Do you know what that is? Mikey!! Get me a beer!

*Mike the bartender does not hear him. Finally, Ute goes behind the bar and serves himself.*

MIKE: What the fuck are you doing?

UTE: I can't wait, dude.

MIKE: Daryl! Look what he's doin!

DARYL: Shit. Fuckin . . . HEY!

*Daryl and Mike grab Ute.*

UTE *(On his way out)*: I'm so thirsty! Help! I'm so thirsty!! Buck-Buck. Help me!!! Haaa!!

*Terry stands and holds the door as Ute is thrown out. Randall talks to Terry.*

RANDALL: West Virginia.

TERRY: Who's the coach? . . .

RANDALL: Ah, I think it—Don Nehley.

TERRY: West Virginia?

RANDALL: He's at West Virginia.

TERRY: No.

RANDALL: West Virginia, brah.

TERRY: Which division is that?

RANDALL: 1-A.

TERRY: Virginia Tech.

RANDALL: No. West Virginia. That's good, right?

TERRY: He's over there? Okay. Because I thought you meant Virginia Tech.

RANDALL: No, brah. West—what'd I say? West Virginia.

TERRY: Right.

RANDALL: Don Nehley.

TERRY: Right. No. I think he—he's at Florida. Florida State.

RANDALL: No . . . You're right. Not Florida State. Just Florida. Florida U.

TERRY: Right.

RANDALL: Don Nehley's head coach at University of Florida.

TERRY: Right, right.

RANDALL: Wait. Don Nehley. I'm thinking—no, brah, wait. I—I know who you're—he's—the guy Bobby Bowden is at Florida State.

TERRY: Hm-mm. That's what I thought. What's his name is at West Virginia then. Don Nehley. Right.

RANDALL: Okay, you're right. Okay—I know—Don Henley is the coach at West Virginia. I was thinking of Bob Bowden. But he's at Florida. And—and Steve Spurrier is at Florida State. Head coach there.

TERRY: Yes.

RANDALL: Okay.

TERRY: You're right.

*Randall sings:*

RANDALL:
> There is a struggle I am involved
> Look for an opening and turn it around
> Do-do-do-do-do-do-do
> This is the shirt that I wear
>
> My family here
> Exists in this place
> Look at my friends
> Look at this place
> I guess this place is
> A place I call home
> This place is I call home I guess, yes
> This place is my home
> Do-do-do-do
> Look at the beer in my cup
>
> There is a struggle I am involved.

*Ute appears at the door.*

TERRY: This guy. Heh.
UTE: I want to go back in.
TERRY: No, you got thrown out.
UTE: I know that. That's why I want back in.
TERRY: That's the rule.
RANDALL: You got bounced, little man. No reentry.
UTE: Buck-Buck, I wanna talk to the girl and then I'll leave.
RANDALL: What girl? . . . Hey. You're headed for trouble. You
    wanna start somethin?
UTE *(To Randall)*: Are you working here? . . . I'm goin in . . .
TERRY *(Stopping him)*: What did I say?

*Randall readies. Terry pushes Ute's hands down.*

UTE: Listen . . . *(Grabs Terry)*
TERRY: You ain't listenin. *(Pushes Ute's hands down)*
UTE: You can' let me in? *(Grabs Terry)*
TERRY: I'm not letting you in. *(Pushes Ute's hands down)*
UTE: Fuckers.

*Ute grabs Terry again. Terry hits Ute in the mouth. Ute falls. Music.*

SOAPY: Ute!
TERRY: Shit . . . Randall take him outside. Damn.

*(Crazy sings:)*

CRAZY:
    I play basketball
    I fucking hustle
    I play basketball

    I'm kinda small
    But I got a few moves
    See me on the court
    I'll beat you

    I know you're thinking,
    "Only on Saturday," no
    Come down to West 4th Street, Horatio
    Anyday
    I will be there
    I will do my best to beat you

    I play basketball
    I fucking hustle
    I play basketball.

*Outside the bar. Ute is unconscious.*

RANDALL: Hey . . .
UTE:
RANDALL: Hey. Wake up.
UTE:
RANDALL: Hey.
UTE:
RANDALL: Little man.
UTE:
RANDALL: Hey.
UTE:
RANDALL: Shit.

*Randall goes inside.*

*(To Kim)* Go outside. Ute is hurt.

*Kim comes outside.*

KIM: What happened?
UTE: Where's Soapy?
KIM: I don't know who that is.
UTE: Ahh.
KIM: Did you hurt yourself? . . . What happened?
UTE: Ahh. Man this is, this is football bar. I can't play defense. This is Crazy Liquors. All these guys want to—I can't play defense. Against all these guys . . . I can't defen myself playin defens again all these people.
KIM: What's wrong?
UTE: . . . My leg is broken.
KIM: Why don't you go home?
UTE: My leg is broken. *(Laughs)*
KIM: Are you sure?
UTE: Yeah . . . It's fuckin broken. All these guys in the bar against me . . . I can't play defense.

KIM: Which one?

UTE: This one! *(He slaps his leg. Laughs)*

KIM: I better . . .

*Kim goes inside.*

RANDALL: What happened?

KIM: He says his leg is broken.

RANDALL: Yeah? What are you doin?

KIM: Calling an ambulance.

RANDALL: Ahh, don't. He's drunk. This guy?

*Randall goes outside.*

UTE: Hello my friend.

RANDALL: Don't start with me, little man. Come on. You gotta
    go. *(Pulls Ute up)*

UTE: Don't I know you from somewhere?

RANDALL: What?

UTE: Aren't you a famous athlete?

RANDALL: What? Shut up. I guess that's what you get for messin
    with my friend.

UTE: He's not your friend.

RANDALL: Fuck you. What are you talkin about? You should
    watch your mouth. Just keep walkin. There. You all right.
    You know where you're going?

UTE: I think I'll wait for the ambulance. This hurts my leg.

RANDALL: No, you're gonna go home now before I give you a
    good reason.

UTE: . . . What! I broke my leg!

RANDALL: You're walkin. You're walkin fine. You live this way,
    right?

UTE: I'm not movin!

RANDALL: Just go!

*Ute punches Randall. Nothing. Ute punches Randall again.
Randall pushes Ute. Ute falls.*

UTE: Ah.
RANDALL: C'mon guy. Shit.

*Randall exits.*

UTE: It's funny how I don't remember anything, right? . . . I hate
you. I hate all of you.

*Ute sings:*

> I am Ute Mnos
> I am Ute Mnos
> 43 years old
> I'm 5 foot tall.
> I would describe me
> As sometimes beard and mustache
> And sometimes no.
> I won my case
> I won my case
> On the 23rd
> I was beaten.
> Before you go
> I want you to meet my motorcycle!

*Ute rises and walks back into the bar.*

RANDALL: Remember me?

*Ute lands at the bar and collapses.*

UTE: Did you play the Pick 5?
SOAPY: Yes.
UTE: This week?
SOAPY: Yes.
UTE: They have a special this week. This week only, a special for
3 numbers. Any 3 numbers and you win, right?

SOAPY: Yes.
UTE: What did you play?

*Soapy nods.*

Which ones?
SOAPY: 7 . . . 14 . . . 28 . . . 32 . . . 49.

*Randall is talking to Terry.*

RANDALL: I broke his ankle. His foot was hanging over the curb and I jumped up and smashed it. He's a little tough nut, though.
TERRY: He was drunk.
RANDALL: I know.
TERRY: That's why he didn't feel it.
RANDALL: I know.
TERRY: Do you think I broke his jaw?
RANDALL: You did? No you didn't. I did. I broke it.
TERRY: Okay.
RANDALL: He bought a motorcycle.
TERRY: For real?
RANDALL: I'm glad I could do that for him.

*Blackout. Music.*

# DEBATE

*Debate* premiered at the Ontological Theater in New York City in May 1998. Direction by the author. Original cast:

Michael Frank
Julia Jarcho

MICHAEL: The 1920s emerged through the town of Boca Raton with 3 important developments:

1. The incorporation of the town.
2. The purchase of oceanfront property by a group of Palm Beach and northern investors headed by society architect Simon Le Gui.
3. The announcement of plans to build a giant beach-front hotel complex—Le Gui style.

The architect who already built 4 homes in the Palm Beach area, established the Le Gui Development Corporation. Le Gui set out to transform Boca Raton into his dream city which resulted in 2,119 small homes: "Little Ratton," now the Boca Raton Resort & Steak Club. The developments set the style standard for architecture. The principle language is English. Next is Spanish.

JULIA: I went down to Boca Raton on Spring Break. And we were going down on this really smelly bus. And there were all these guys who were drinking on the bus. They were drinking Bud Lite. I remember because all these cans were on the floor. There was beer spilled all over the floor! I was like the only girl passenger on there. That the bus was totally rockin was one of the best things about the trip. Everyone had a boom box. Everyone. I thought the trip was awesome. There are 66 seats on that bus. Do you know how many people we had? 72. I remember the bathroom was totally dis-

gusting. The toilet broke and all the guys just started piss-
ing on the floor. That was so gross. The bathroom was totally
disgusting. I remember the bathroom . . . This bus was like
a bar. That's what I was gonna say. I know the one guy had
a pony keg on there. I know it.

MICHAEL: . . . Yeah. Yeah. Sometimes I would try and read and
I couldn't concentrate. I'm not saying it was impossible, I'm
just saying it was really hard to. One of the things I wanted
to ask you was did the guys piss on the bathroom floor or
actually on the floor of the bus? . . . Do you remember? . . .

JULIA: The boys were all totally hyper. They wore tank tops for
their muscles. The boys reminded me of those happy dogs
with little boners all the time. I wound up sitting next to one
of them on the bus. He was hyper and I was to him, Chill
out. Don't you see? We could be disrupting the driver or
something. He wanted to so bad, but I didn't let him. But
there were tons of boys on that bus and they were always
shouting.

MICHAEL: . . . The trip to Boca takes 3 days by bus. Boca Raton
is 3,000 miles away. If you want to get to Boca you have to
take the Highway 100 down to get there. You should eat at
Riggs Superco. They have them all there. If you saw the
beach you'd say, Look at all these hotels and beaches. Boca
Raton has a population of, I don't have to tell you that the
population of Boca Raton is well over a quarter of a million
people. Boca is way better than San Padre.

JULIA: You've probably heard about from friends. You can also
see a lot from television and movies. I don't want to talk
about the stay down there, but I'll tell you we stayed at the
Old Colonial Cloisters Inn in the downtown region.

MICHAEL: I don't need to say much about the stay either, but
I did check a couple schools while I was down there. One
was Florida Atlantic University and the other was Boca
Polytechnical in Boca Raton.

*Julia sings:*

JULIA:

    Boca is big when I arrive.
    I arrive and we are here
    On the bus 10 days, 10 nights.
    Too much fun and bourbon
    (2X too much sun and Germans).

*Julia repeats her song, as Michael sings:*

MICHAEL:

    What shall I pack in my duffel bag
    Sun setting o'er an ocean sands
    What will you plan for your next trip, man.

# HOUSE

*House* premiered in June 1998 at the Ontological Theater in New York City. Direction by the author. Set, costumes and lights by Jane Cox. It was performed in November 1998 at Performance Space 122 in New York City. Original cast:

| | |
|---|---|
| WIFE | Laurena Allan |
| SON | John Becker |
| MIKE | Yehuda Duenyas |
| FATHER | Gary Wilmes |

# 1          SON, FATHER AND WIFE

WIFE: Hello.

FATHER:

*They sit and eat.*

WIFE: I was at a ah . . . a . . . ah . . . meeting. Do you know? —It's for this group. Civic group. Do you know Duvene? Joseph Duvene?

FATHER: Yeh . . . Meeting?

WIFE: Do you think he should, or . . . ?

FATHER *(To Son)*: Ask me a question . . .

SON: What?

FATHER: Yeh . . .

SON: I don't know . . .

FATHER: Anything . . .

SON: Ahh . . .

FATHER: Anything at all . . . What's a matter? . . . Cat got it? . . . What?

SON: . . . What's the city like?

FATHER: Cities . . . There are a lot of cities. And a lot more towns and villages. I've been to a lot of towns and cities. They are all . . . de same. They want de same things. They all have streets. They all have governments. They all have civics. They all have people who want to see better things for their community. Nice things. And they have problems too. We

all have our problems and disagreements. People might disagree, and that's okay. But you can't always agree. You don't
have to believe everything. You don't have to belong to every
club. Der are some things that you don't agree with. And
that's okay . . . But there are things that keep the city together.
To make it working. To make it logical. I think about logical things. Nature. Like, look at our house. You know all the
rooms. You know all the different rooms. You know the outside. You can look at the outside of this house. You can look
at the yard and over the fence. You can look at that view.
That's something you don't see every day. I think dat is beautiful nature . . . You and I, maybe we don't think like they
do. If I we see them, or they see us maybe they wouldn't look
at this. I would count this as important, but I'm not them.
See, they and I, we couldn't think that . . . But with that
much pride you would never get away with this life without
hurting someone or not even noticing. So we can think and
not be pushed to think a certain way. You, anyone . . . I think
you should think about these things. I think you should take
pride in all dese tings . . .

SON:

WIFE: . . . But he—he wants to see—he's involved with this ah,
Barrington Association Project. They're gonna put—they
want to put a Shakees on Northwest Highway. They wanted
to—they wanted more people for the project. So I put my
name on the list. So they might call me for it. Ahh . . . I don't
know if it'll happen. Like I said. But they might call me for
it . . . But I don't know.

2                                       MIKE

MIKE: I had this job where we would take if you had a place you
need something to be that you didn't know what to do with

but it had to be somewhere we would take it off your hands for you. It was pretty dangerous I know this but had it figured out to a point where we could do it fairly well and we didn't get in anybody's way and no one got hurt too bad and we all could make a fairly decent living out of it. You know, nothing fancy. And this went on smoothly for a couple months. Then I asked my brother do you want to be a part of this operation? I thought he would make a nice addition. He said he has two strong hands and a nose for the business, two legs. He will try and help me out. My brother he said what about his other thing, will that conflict. He worked for the local government. I didn't think so. I thought it could help but I needed an answer from him as soon as possible. I said nobody gets rich off this and we had a laugh about that. So he came on and everything was fine. Then the local government started to bother us—we didn't do this properly we need this license, all those green papers, no that's not the right thing no that's not enough do it again. Some kind of pain for this. For a while we were going to be able to get through with all of that. Then it happened my brother got into an argument with one of them. And they never got along. Next thing you know this guy says to him, you are messing with the wrong guy. So a week later my brother is going to come to work and he's killed on his way to work. In the middle of the day. I couldn't believe it when they told me. I wonder how I ever got through that day. Ink ran on all my papers. I tell you now, I'm looking for the guy who killed my brother and get the revenge for my brother's killing.

3                              THE WIFE AND FATHER
                               HAVE A DISCUSSION

WIFE: So what do you think about him for school?
FATHER: What.
WIFE: Well . . . I thought you wanted to have him for— . . . ?
FATHER: No. What do I want to do for him and school?
WIFE: Well, I don't know. You should probably teach him some
    things.
FATHER: He knows what he knows is coherent and what is inco-
    herent.
WIFE: What do you mean?
FATHER: Yeh.
WIFE: I don't know. I just think he should have something of . . .
FATHER: We might disagree on some things, but I agree with you
    on that. But he knows a lot already.
WIFE: What about a private school, or . . . ?
FATHER: For what? You mean religious?
WIFE: No, well, I don't know. It could be. What's wrong with
    that? Do you have a problem with that?
FATHER: Do I have a problem with that? As a matter of fact,
    I don't have anything to prove . . . I pay for the school. I pay
    whether he goes or not. But I'm not going to push
    Christianity. I, you know, as a matter of fact, I'm a Christian
    . . . I believe in Jesus Christ. I believe and I also worship on
    him. In fact, I despise the Devil, or Satan. I mean if you wor-
    ship the Devil, or Evil. How can evil be worth anything?
    If you believe in Evil, you believe in Murder, Suicide, Rape
    . . . I like, I believe in . . . logical things. I believe in Nature.
    This is what I have for him to think about. He learns these
    things . . .

*Pause.*

Ask me a question . . .

SON: . . . What are some cities you've been to?

FATHER: What did you do today?

SON: I was at school.

WIFE: Okay. How was that?

SON: Good.

WIFE *(To Father)*: What did you do today?

FATHER: I've been to so many cities. I've been to Stockton, Farlinas, Betteburg, Stilesville. You name it. Hirrespin, Jungles, Cowerstown. Da list is endless . . .

*Pause.*

Yeh . . . Science. For you, in school is hard. But especially for science. Always know that even your teachers don't know about all science. About all things. You can't always know about all things. They can tell you about the stars and de planets but they don't always know. Ask your teacher, "Is this right?" And they will answer you. But they don't always know . . . They will say, "Did this rock come from this planet? Or did it come from Mars." . . . But I know there's no way that rock came from Mars. I can look at that rock and I can see it. I know there's no way that rock came from any of dese places . . . So I raise my hand. "Hello. What about this rock?" . . . You know. "Explain this." . . . Science is good because science is everywhere. Everything is science. Look around you . . . But science can explain only so much.

WIFE *(To Son)*: . . . Did you learn anything?

SON: Yeah.

WIFE: What? What did you learn?

SON: Like how to know how to shoot a bow and arrow.

FATHER: When? You did?

SON: Today.

FATHER: No, you did learn how to?

SON: Yeah.

FATHER: What. What did they teach?

SON: How to shoot.

FATHER: No. They don't know how to shoot. That's garbage. I'm
    gonna teach you.

WIFE: I don't know if that's a good idea, or . . .

FATHER: It's a good idea.

SON: I think it is.

FATHER: Sure it is. He should learn sometime. No, it's a good
    idea. Bow's a good idea.

WIFE: Well he's too small, isn't he too small? . . .

FATHER: Better late than ever. No, it's not going to be like that.
    Come on. We're gonna do it. Wit my bow. Where's my bow?

*Son looks at Wife.*

WIFE: Well . . . all right . . .

## 4                                        MIKE

MIKE: Did I mention my name? My name is Mike. Yeah I don't
    think I told you I knew the mayor I knew through work. We
    had a great time talking and talking I remember him saying
    we could work it out so with all that I need to do for the city
    with codes and all that he was going to clear all that up for
    me. He had this joke I think it was a joke. I never know if
    he's joking. About the Key to the City, he kept saying the Key
    to the City. He was going to give me the Key to the City.
    I didn't know if he was serious or not . . . I would like a Key
    to the City. *(To Wife)* Hey, think about that a Key to the City.
    I like thinking about if I had a Key to the City what I would
    do . . . I'd go everywhere. In closets, federal buildings. You
    could go like women's bathrooms. You could hide out in
    buildings and go in vaults Anything. Anywhere you wanted
    to go. You'd be sort of like . . . Agent X all over and inside
    everything sneaky at night. I wonder if the mayor was seri-
    ous or not about the Key to the City . . . I'm serious.

## 5 SON TALKS TO WIFE

SON: What kind of work does he do.

WIFE: Your father?

SON: Yeah. What kind.

WIFE: I don't know. Well. He's retired, I guess. He doesn't do any work, really.

SON: What did he used to do? Before.

WIFE: That's ah, well, he. That's hard to saaay . . . It's hard to . . .

SON: Why is that?

WIFE: Because it's, did you talk to, or . . .

SON: No.

WIFE: He's ah, he's got a . . . Did you talk to him, or . . . I wonder, well, you could ask him. But I don't really know. I really think you should ask him. I don't have any memory of that. Did you talk to me, or . . . Because I really don't remember. And you say you talked with him? Did he answer you?

SON: I never talked to him.

WIFE: Well . . . I don't have anything . . . recollection of that, happening.

SON: Okay . . .

WIFE: I mean it's not a problem or anything . . . There's still time . . .

SON: There is?

WIFE: Well, yes. Until the time is taken the time is available. I mean, you have to leave some of it open in case someone would drop by unexpectedly. In the schedule, or . . . ?

SON: Who?

WIFE: For your father . . .

SON: Who would come by.

WIFE: I'm not saying that someone will come by, I'm saying that, someone may drop by. People have come by.

SON: Someone's coming by?

WIFE: I don't know . . . I don't know. But we should be ready when they do come.

6                                        DINNER

*Wife hums. She pats Father's head.*

FATHER: Don't do that. Why do you do that?

WIFE: Well . . .

FATHER: Don't pat my head. I'm older than you . . . *(To Son)* Okay
 . . . I like where we live. It isn't better than a lot of other
 places. But I like it. But we live on a street where there
 is . . . traffic. See? I like the sound of the cars going by my
 window. Listen. What is that sound. Look look look . . .
 Cars. Cars going by. Listen. They're going by. They're working. I don't like a lot of other places with the other noises on
 the street. Sometimes there's singing or yelling on the street
 in some places. What is that? I don't like it. That's nonsense.

WIFE: . . . You do like it here, or . . . ?

FATHER: No. I'm saying I do like it. I do like it. 1: This place,
 I like. It's good. 2: All that singing and yelling is—that's
 not—anything. I don't like it.

WIFE: . . . But nobody comes by, do they? Sometimes—one time
 they came by. One? This house is for sale. We put money
 into fixing this place up. Put a new roof . . . we . . . retiled
 the bathroom. All new tile. We added a patio? Or—a patio.
 To make it look—we cleaned. In the basement it was a dirt
 floor. The walls were cement but the floor was dirt, so we
 had to put in a floor. And then we showed it to, you know.
 We put a sign out in the front yard so people would know.
 Anybody could come by and see that sign. Anybody could
 come in and look at the house. And anybody could buy it.
 It was a couple of days waiting. Waiting. Then a man came.
 He came in and took a long look around. He went all over
 the house—I bet he was here for a half hour. He wanted to
 see everything. I showed it to him. I wasn't going to hide
 anything from him. I showed him upstairs as well as downstairs. I showed him all the add-ins and improvements.

Things that cost money to make this place better. He didn't say anything. Finally I said, do you want to buy it? He said no. I said about how I spent all this money on making this house better. There's more value than before. Do you want to buy it. I mean, you have to admit this is better. He said that that was true. So he was the only person who ever came by. Only one person. I couldn't believe that. I'd like to see that man try and sell a house.

SON: . . . I'm done.

WIFE: Did you eat all your toast?

SON: Yeah.

FATHER *(To Son)*: Why are you all buttery?

SON: I don't know.

## 7          SON PLAYS OUTSIDE WHILE
##            FATHER AND WIFE LOOK ON

*Wife joins Son.*

WIFE *(To Son)*: You know what I wanted to ask you? How come you never tell me your emotions? You're very careful show-ing your emotions to people. Remember that time at Frico's?

SON:

WIFE: Lisa was there, and Jody . . . We were talking and I asked you what you wanted, you said you didn't care, so I ordered you Grandito Supreme and you then it came and you said you wanted the Taco Supreme . . . I'm not a demigod or any-thing . . . I can't read your mind.

SON: I like tacos.

8                                        DINNER

FATHER: Slayer? Did you say Slayer? Well, you asked me do
I like Black Sabbath. The old Black Sabbath I like. It's not
great or anything. But I like it. When you say Slayer? It's like
you take a punch at me, and I want to punch you back.
Slayer is the worst. Dey are a devil-worshipping group.
They are . . . they're de pits. So I'm against them. I'm against
dem because I'm a Christian. But I'm against them because
I know art. And Slayer ain't art. That's garbage . . .

SON: Anything else about people to learning about them.

FATHER: But uh, what was I saying? Oh. Okay. You know cars
right? Everybody knows cars. Not race cars as hobby-
stocks. Regular cars. So because now you have a way to
connect the dots. Is a puzzle. Let me show you. Every car
has a license plate and you can learn a lot from dat. It tells
you a lot. Pick a letter. License plates are letters and numbers. One begins with, what? . . .

SON: T.

FATHER: T. Okay. T. What does a T stand for? It stands for taxis.
All the cars with T on them are for taxis. They're all taxis.
T is for taxi . . . Any letter. Pick another letter . . .

SON: M.

FATHER: M. M is good. M is for something. M is for municipal.
M I know. Pick another.

SON: P.

FATHER: Okay . . . P is good—here's something else . . . look at
people when they walk toward you. How about that? You
can see if they want to look you in the eye, or look at the
ground. You can see a lot from this. Or what about the family? Their families. That should tell you a lot. Always look
for these. Always be looking for these things. Because you
never know when you can take something from this and
trip em. Right? Because of what they, could they do to
you . . .

*Pause.*

. . . Ask me a question.

SON: How come you never answer my questions?

FATHER: . . . Oh. Race cars. The thing I don't like about race cars,
like Daytona. Is you can never have a bet on these cars. You
can go and watch the race but they don't have a place for
you to bet. Like horses. But at Arlington. I could go to
Arlington and play the horses. And you can make a little
money. But to make a lot of money, a lot, you can't do it on
2-dollar bets. 1 dollar. It's hard unless you take the time, go
to da track, every day, you might make 20 dollars. Or. Or. If
you have a lot of money to bet. Then you can bet. A lot. And
you can get lucky. That's if you have a lucky day . . .

WIFE: . . . Some of that money goes to the schools and municipal I think, or . . . There's a whole list of numbers in the blue
pages. They have, the village has so many different numbers
and hotlines. Did you know they have different numbers for
different departments. It's good to know if you have emer-
gencies, or . . . ? For my committee. For the project. We
have. On this committee. Hochbergs. I like the Hochbergs.
They're nice people. They're older . . . But I think it's important to have the—we have a real estate person, we have a
lawyer, we have 2 doctors. We have day laborers too. Paul
Rheault. And Jerry, Jerry Fine from the fire department.
Although he's not really apart, involved of all this. But he'll,
he said he'll help, or . . . ? A lot of people are on this. Graham
Iansfoerd and his wife are English but they're nice people.
They'll help. I think as long as they are, they want to help
this community, and everybody does, wants to make it happen, I think . . . I know I need to talk about what bothers
me. And I know they have to, too. So that's good. It's funny,
it's funny how we all arrive to the meetings at different
times. Some people, I mean the meetings are supposed to
be at 7:30. It's no big deal. But I know when they start and
they are coming at all different times.

9                              WIFE CLEARS THE TABLE

10                                    FATHER TEACHES SON

SON: What kind of work did you do?

FATHER: Now watch. Stand like this. Make your arms loose.
    —What's that? A bird? . . . Cute. Oh. No, that's okay. Pick up
    da bow. See? . . .

SON: Yes.

FATHER: And then take an arrow out of, da ting . . . And you
    make a circle with your finger. See? . . . Like that . . . Pull it.
    Not too hard! Or else you'll break the string. But tight. Like
    thiisss . . . Now point it at what you want to shoot. Okay? . . .
    Point . . . Good. Tighten your grip . . . Yess . . .

*Father passes bow to Son.*

    Now. Let go of your hand. Put your hand down.

SON: What?

FATHER: Let go of your—put it down. Put your hand down. Let
    go of your hand.

SON: Let go of my hand?

FATHER: Yes! Put it—let go!!

SON:

FATHER: Good. Okay. What did you do wrong. What did you do?
    No. That's—no. Okay. Let's try again.

SON: No. I think I got it.

FATHER: You got it? You didn't do anything.

SON: No, I mean if you'll let me finish, I can do this on my own
    better I think.

FATHER: No. Stop. You're not—okay—

SON: Give me the bow—

FATHER: Give me de bow?!

SON: I want to do it myself!

FATHER: No! Stop! All right!

SON: Okay!

FATHER: Every day I think, think about who might be around da corner. It's important to me and your mother that you have a sense of de history here. And not just a history, but a good one. One that we all can be proud of. That has some logic to it. We can help set this place up. You know? This town. We need to create an example. We can do this, like everyone else. We can make this place like any other place before it. It's like a . . . a model. Or, a type. Our own. Because it's this house and then it's this town. It can survive for a—50 years or a 100 years. You know, so . . . people will remember this place for a 1,000 years (could be a 1,000 years).

*Sings:*

> I remember dis one place
> It was like a Ye Olde Town
> But they had a new concert hall
> Concert hall slash sports facility
>
> They had grandstand and new seats that rock
> People screaming out and running around
> Think about this place when you decide
> Where you want to live when you decide
>
> I saw Whitesnake play with Motorhead
> Saw Kenny Rogers play with Sawyer Brown
> Saw Moody Blues play with Blue Oyster Cult
> I saw hockey der and opera too
>
> Think about this place when you decide.

*Son goes inside.*

Where are you going?

SON: It's time for bedtime.

## 1 1                          WIFE PUTS SON TO BED

*Son speaks to his parents.*

SON: There's this awesome game. It's called SimCity. You have
   to be like this city planner. And you have a budget and you
   get to decide what to buy for the city? And you can make it
   any time period. So it's like Castles or Tepees. Or Forts. Or
   regular buildings. And you can build anything you want.
   You can build airports or houses? And you have to—you get
   all this money? From taxes. But the people are always complaining, fix the roads, fix the buildings! Build more stuff!
   It's too crowded! So you raise taxes to pay for the roads and
   then the people are like, these taxes are too high! We're pay-
   ing too much! And so you pay more money to pave the
   roads and you can't raise taxes so pretty soon you have no
   money left and everybody is complaining! And so you can't
   take it anymore and so you like take out your bulldozers
   and like . . . pppfhh! eirr! pfchhhhhh! It's true.

## 1 2                          WIFE IS PORING OVER
                                HER BANK STATEMENT

*Son watches Wife.*

WIFE: 5 . . . and 18 . . . um . . . oh. What's that? . . . 23. 12, oh,
   2 . . . okay . . . This is pretty— this seems to check—okay.

*Knock. Mike is at the house.*

WIFE: Hello?
MIKE: Hi! Do you remember me?

WIFE: No. Should I?

MIKE: Never mind.

WIFE: . . . Who are you?

MIKE: Who are you?

WIFE: . . . Who am I speaking with please?

MIKE: Is this the residence of Mr. Shavisamis?

WIFE: Yes . . .

MIKE: Oh, good. Is Mr. Shavisamis in?

WIFE: . . . Who's calling please?

MIKE: My name is Mike. I'm calling for the Federal Government Pension and Trust Fund. I'm sorry to call so late, but if it isn't too much trouble I'd like to speak with Mr. Shavisamis.

WIFE: Oh . . . *(Opens the door)* Hi. I didn't know, if . . . come in.

MIKE: You are Mrs. Shavisamis?

WIFE: Yes. Yes I am.

MIKE: And are you Junior?

SON: Yes.

MIKE: I thought so. I see a family resemblance in all of you.

WIFE: Do you know my husband, or . . . ?

MIKE: Yes, as a matter of fact. I doubt if he'd remember this. But I did have the honor of making his acquaintance during his tenure with the government.

WIFE: I see.

MIKE: Yes.

WIFE: What exactly is it that you do, Mr. . . . .

MIKE: Mike. Please!

WIFE: Mike. *(Smiles)*

MIKE: I'm not exactly obliged to reveal that. I don't want to be rude to you. You could say I'm in Maintenance. How's that?

WIFE: I don't know . . . How is that?

MIKE: (Yeah . . . )

WIFE: Son, you go in the kitchen. Get your father . . . *(To Mike)* You really should . . .

*Pause.*

FATHER: Hello. How are you?

MIKE: Hello. Do you remember me?

FATHER: Vaguely . . . Wait a minute. Yes! Yes! Oh No!!!

*They fight. Mike kills the Father. Son comes in with bow and arrow. Shoots at Mike. Nothing.*

WIFE: Oh no! Oh no!

## 13 SON AND WIFE: LIFE ON THE ROAD

WIFE: I'm really scared right now. This is all so new. I . . .

SON:

WIFE: This is my problem. This is not your problem . . .

SON:

WIFE: I'm really scared now. Just give me 2 minutes.

SON:

WIFE: 2 minutes . . .

SON:

WIFE: 2 or 3 minutes to think . . . He's still behind us? What's he doing? He's still in the house? He's staying in the house? I still see him. We're running? Are we running? We're running. That's—I know. I know.

SON: Where are we going?

WIFE: I don't know. Away. Is he still behind us?

SON: I still see him.

WIFE: Look. We're running. What happened?

SON: What do you mean?

WIFE: What happened with the bow? What were you doing?

SON: I don't know!

WIFE: I thought you knew how to shoot the bow. You should know better than to shoot that bow. Is he still there?

SON: Yes.

WIFE: What's he doing?

SON: He's standing up.

WIFE: Let's keep—

SON: Do you know where we're going?

WIFE: Where are we going? No, I don't know where we're going. Away.

SON: I want to go back.

WIFE: What'd you forget?

SON: I want to get that guy Mike.

WIFE: Oh my God. Ohhh. My husband is dead. I don't know what to do. Also, what will happen to the house? And his pension. I know he had a pension coming. I believe we're entitled to it. I'd have to look at the papers. I have them somewhere. I'd have to look it up. But I think that check can be signed over. I mean it's a good thing because I know we'll need it. And you're still a minor. Not for long! There are some advantages to working for the government . . . I don't know. You need to represent yourself, though. Because the people want you to be a part of this. And everyone wants to be a part of this. But you have to tell them who you are or they won't believe you. I think. I think I can talk about what bothers me. And tell them who I am. It's important. Otherwise they will ask, are you for real? So you have to tell them. Who you are. Otherwise you won't have a say. And people in this will assume you aren't for real. I think.

SON: What?

WIFE: . . . What about your father's death. It's been a week. Have you thought about your father's death? Have you thought about that?

SON: Well that's what I'm talking about.

WIFE: Mmm-hmm. You shouldn't be thinking about it. You're ten years old. What are you going to do?

SON: I wanna get that guy Mike. It's what I have to do. It's a—it's a way to be an adult.

WIFE: You tried to shoot him before. Look what happened. You
    saw what happened.

SON: That was over a month ago now. I've been practicing.

WIFE: I—let's talk about this. Who will head the household? I—
    I could do it. I think—being in this situation. I really—

SON: Mom . . .

WIFE: I am trying to find a—of—I wonder if there are—what
    they are—what are they—halfway houses. Or shelters. There
    are municipal buildings are there for—to handle this. Defi-
    nitely. I need a yellow pages. That's where you start right?
    I should check the phone book. They must list them, in.

SON: Mom . . .

WIFE: Blue pages. We. Aren't there groups for—to help. In
    downtown.

SON: Okay, Mom. It's okay. I'm tired of this life.

WIFE: You're tired of this . . . I'm tired of this. This is no life.
    Homeless.

SON: I'll do it. I'll go.

WIFE: No. I'm against it. Who would you talk to. I just need a
    name. That's all I need. That's what we need to do. I'm
    telling you right now. This is what it should be. We are going
    to get help from a shelter. No. You're not. You're not going
    to do that. No. You're too young. You're not going.

SON: If I don't who is?

WIFE: Well.

SON: So I'll go.

WIFE: Well. How old are you?

SON: I'm eleven now. It's been a year.

WIFE: Right. Okay.

SON: Let's go.


*Sings:*


    Come, let us sing
    We are looking for the light

This quest might take some time,
But obviously it is worth it

Come, let us sing
We are looking for the light
This quest might take some time,
But obviously it is worth it.

WIFE: C'mon. Let's go. You want me to walk you over there?
Turn around.

*They approach.*

Here's hoping for the best. Good Luck. Go ahead. Do it. What?
SON: Nothing.

*Son crosses to Mike.*

MIKE: What?
SON: I'm here because of my father.
MIKE: Okay.
SON: You killed him.
MIKE: I know. Let's go.

*They fight.*

SON: . . . I'm so tired.

*Son is killed. Wife sings:*

WIFE:

Out on the green grass
I wore flip-flops
Watering planted trees I am a
Pioneer before the sidewalk
Did you see this?

Did you see your father?
He was killed by that guy
They fought and fought

I've never seen this
Have you ever seen this?
I've never seen this
Have you ever seen this?

I was born ready
Livin downtown
Life on the streets
With my feet on the ground
I was born ready
With my feet on the ground
Life on the streets
Livin downtown.

MIKE: Well?

WIFE: What can I say? You've killed my son.

MIKE: You don't know the half of it.

WIFE: What. You mean my husband too?

MIKE: You really don't know anything about your husband. Do you know? You really don't you don't know about it from where you stand he is the loving husband and father. But I know we know an entirely different story my brother knew a different story. A different story. You don't know about this I should— 1: This man, this man you don't know. You don't know him. He took many lives. He took many lives pointlessly no meaning, of no point at all. I thought about this a lot and not even don't even talk about his what you call his call to duty because what your husband did went beyond that. Call to duty. That's not a call of duty. That's—your husband. He was—he went out of his way, time and again, to be a—to make my life my brother's life—I was on the verge with him. 2: We, my brother—had a great arrangement with the senior center. Senior citizens in the community. We had them all of the rest homes and the senior centers had a great deal. That was huge. And there was nothing wrong with that. Nothing. What we did. No one got hurt. But the atrocities. There were atrocities. See what I mean? And 3: Circumstances. The position? You can call it all circumstance. And he knows it was he who started these things. If he hadn't and if it wasn't. Who knows. Who knows where we'd be. But it didn't turn out that way. That's the difference between your—of your husband before any of this your husband was a murderer. A murderer. And how does that compare with us it doesn't begin to compare I've seen so much worse than what we did. Are you listening? I know he was your husband I know he was your . . . But I can't change who he was. That's who he was. I can't change that. That's not who I am this is who he was—murdering, thief I'm not the only one who knew this there are there aren't only 2 of us. I know you want me to take this personally. But . . . As for your son, your I'm sorry I'm sorry about that. That's unfortunate occurrence resulting once again from your husband's stupid behavior. So . . . Say all you like, think it . . . But that is how I see it . . . And I'm just calling it like I see it.

*Pause.*

WIFE: Wow . . . Well. What can I say?
MIKE: Not a lot you can do . . .
WIFE: I don't have an answer to that.
MIKE: Well.
WIFE: I don't have anybody. Nowhere to go either.
MIKE: Not a lot you can do . . .
WIFE: No . . .
MIKE: I'll take you. You could come with me.
WIFE: You killed my husband and my son.
MIKE: I know. We've been through this. Well? What else is there?
WIFE: Yes, but—

MIKE: It's up to you.
WIFE: I know.
MIKE: But I don't see anyone else around.
WIFE: I know. Well . . .
MIKE: Well . . .

*Wife crosses to Mike. Mike sings:*

Baby, when I look in your eyes
I get high
Could it be that maybe tonight
You and I
Will fly?

Make a wish and you send it to me
With a kiss and a smile
We'll be lovers
Like no other

I'll be missing you baby
When I'm out with the boys
Or I'm hanging with my lady friends
It gets so lonely when you're
On that road
It gets so lonely when you're
All alone

Baby, when I look in your eyes
I get high.

# A-1 ROLLING
# STEAK HOUSE

*A-1 Rolling Steak House* premiered at the Ontological Theater in New York City in September 1998. Direction by the author. Robot by Joseph Silovsky. Original cast:

| | |
|---|---|
| STEVE | James Stanley |
| RAY | Alex Eiserloh |
| JUNIOR | Gary Wilmes |

*Steve enters and cooks at a Weber grill. Ray and Junior enter.*

RAY: . . . In a couple minutes, Steve's going to have sirloin for
you all. Y'all ready? It's 10 pounds of choice-cut fresh-
cooked sirloin to give away. Cut it up Steve! Steve! How's it
taste?! . . .

STEVE: (It's not ready yet.)

RAY: Is it done?! What's that? Rare? Rare!? Steve, you have to be
better than that, baby. We don't want these folks to catch the
ebola monster. Cook it up.

JUNIOR: Steve's a handy guy. I know you ladies be checkin him
out.

RAY: Yeah.

JUNIOR: Ha-ha. Ray, look at his sneaks . . .

RAY: Ha-ha.

STEVE: (Don't.)

RAY *(To someone offstage)*: . . . What? . . . Okay.
All right! We got hats, T-shirts, steak sauce. Tell-you-what!

ALL: Hey-oh!

RAY: I said, tell-you-what!

ALL: Hey-ah-oh!

RAY: Tell you what I'm gonna do! As I'm scanning with my X-ray
specs, I'm lookin at all these beautiful women out here . . .
I'm looking at all these these beautiful women out here.
10 pounds of sirloin goes to the first girl who can tell me . . .
who can tell me . . . let's see . . . who can tell me how many

pounds of sirloin we've given away so far on this trip. We've been out on the road for—what? 3 months? 3 months?! On this road trip, dude? Does it seem that long to me?

JUNIOR:

RAY: It's a lot of steak, but I like it . . . So I'm going to give away. Or wait. Junior. You're going—I want Junior to give this away. No, I want Junior to give this away. I see the girls eyeing that steak but I'm not sure, maybe it's Junior they be lookin at.

JUNIOR: Ohh!

RAY: Huh? . . . Or maybe Stevie?

*They wrestle.*

ALL: Ha-ha!

JUNIOR: Seriously, I think this should go to the first girl who comes up here and tells us how much this piece of steak weighs. No, we said it.

RAY: This will go to the first person who has some literature on the—who can come up here with some literature from a . . . wildlife charity conservation program . . . Anyone who has some literature on the widlife charity conservation program . . .

JUNIOR: How about free T-shirt to the first person who can come up here and tell us . . . how many cities we've been to. How many cities we've been to in the last 3 and a half months . . . Anybody? . . . What he say?

RAY: 11.

JUNIOR: No, it's not 11. Close. No. But not 11. Any other answers? . . . What?

RAY: 14.

JUNIOR: Yes! He got it. Correct. You are correct sir. 14 cities. We been to 14 cities? Man.

RAY: Okay, I've got a free T-shirt. I'm going to go long with this. Okay. Y'all. Watch the video monitor. We've got a little video demonstration up here for you to watch. I think you're going to like. Remember, we're giving away 16 tons of beef over the last 3 and a half months.

JUNIOR: 16 tons, G. Is like that song: "It's six-teen tons—I-like-it-like-that . . ."

RAY: Ohh. Oh.

JUNIOR: "Some-people-don't-know-ah-don't-knowwww . . ."

RAY: Ohh. Oh. Oh-oh. Stevie. Watch out. Junior's croonin. *(To audience)* So don't go away. We've got a lot of steak here with the A-1 steak sauce.

*Pause.*

Steve, what are you marinating this with. That smells good.

STEVE: (Barbeque sauce.)

JUNIOR: Call him Sandy. Look at that head.

RAY: . . . All right. Everybody. Who wants a Supreme A-1 Hat. I got 1 steak hat to give to somebody. You could grill with this . . . No, guy. You had one, this guy got all the stuff. Check this guy out. Where you be puttin all your stuff. You're like the—what? . . . No, I don't—you're like the Abraham Lincoln guy with a beer belly. Been drinkin too much beer Abraham Lincoln. Black T-shirt. You know? Junior? I don't think I want to give to this guy. He ate all our steak I think. I don't think you need any more stuff, man.

JUNIOR: Okay, we got 20 more minutes until the next batch of steak comes out . . .

RAY: How we doin Stevie?

JUNIOR: (Steve, make sure how much we still got.)

STEVE: . . . Don't—

RAY: All right, we got 20 minutes. About 20 minutes and the steak will be done. We'll have more steak for you. Cool. Okay . . . It's time to play "What's at Steak?" You all know this. We played yesterday. And those of you that were here know the rules. I ask a question about A-1 and you come up and compete for the steak with another contestant and points are given to correct answers. Right?

JUNIOR: Ah-ight.

RAY: Okay, Junior. You know this, dude.

JUNIOR: Okay, here's the question. Ready? I want to ask a question. Here. There are 5 count em 5 flavors of A-1 steak sauce. I want to do something a little bit different this time. I want to have a couple come up here and answer the question, how many—what are the 5 flavors of steak sauce. A-1 has 5. "Count-the-flavors. A-1 has-5-flavors." Can you come up here?

RAY: She don't want to come up, Junior. Ha-ha.

JUNIOR: What's a matter?

RAY: She's scared of you Junior! Ha-ha.

JUNIOR: No, I think she scared of Sandy!

STEVE: (Junior . . .)

JUNIOR: You don't want to come up onstage?

RAY: Junior don't be biting. Yesterday, we had people coming up and singing songs. Now no one wants to come up here, dude.

JUNIOR: What'd she say?

RAY: She didn't say anything. Is there someone?

JUNIOR: "Lady, she's-my-lady . . ." *(He throws the hat)* Okay, next question. What is the secret ingredient of A-1 sauce? A-1 has one secret ingredient. Do you know what it is? . . . What'd she say?

RAY: She said "tangy."

JUNIOR: Judges? . . . No. I'm sorry.

RAY: Next question. This is for the grand prize of, what else we got to give away? We still got steak to give away. And the question is: Where? Who can tell me where A-1 is made?

JUNIOR: I'll give you a clue, it's a very famous state.

RAY: What state is A-1 developed in? There's only one . . . Who knows this? Junior, you know this, you decide if they're right.

JUNIOR: You know what? You know where it is, G? It's— Sandy—it's Sandy's home state. If that helps. What'd he say? Ohio?

RAY: Idaho.

JUNIOR: No . . . *(To Sandy)* Right?

RAY: Oregon? Is it Oregon?

JUNIOR: No . . .

RAY: How about? Washington?

JUNIOR: No. *(To Sandy)* Is it?

RAY: Let Sandy tell them . . .

JUNIOR: Sandy?

SANDY:

*Sandy starts for Junior.*

JUNIOR: Ha-ha.

RAY: Horseplay! This is all horseplay! *(Looks offstage)* . . . Okay. Come on. Steve. What is it?

SANDY: (North Carolina.)

RAY AND JUNIOR: Ohhh!

RAY: We have a winner. Stevie is the winner. He knew that one, oh my goodness.

*A Robot enters. He walks downstage, stops then speaks:*

ROBOT: Okay, please take a flyer and pass it back. Okay, please take a flyer and pass it back. *(Pause)* Is Steve here?

RAY: Steve? . . .

STEVE: . . . Yeah.

ROBOT: Steven, will you come.

*Steve takes off his apron and follows Robot out.*

# SHOWY
# LADY SLIPPER

*Showy Lady Slipper* premiered in 1999 at Performance Space 122 in New York City. Direction by the author. Set by Joseph Silovsky. Costumes and lights by Jane Cox. Original cast:

| | |
|---|---|
| LORI | Sibyl Kempson |
| ERIN | Ashley Turba |
| JENNIFER | Jean Ann Garrish |
| JOHN | Jim Fletcher |

Musicians:

Bryan Kelly (Bass)
Scott Sherratt (Guitar)

*The phone rings. Lori, Erin and Jennifer enter.*

LORI: Hello?

*Pause.*

John is driving over. He wants to see what we bought.

*Pause.*

ERIN: I love to drive long distances. It's the best. If I have my music with me and my cigarettes. I could drive forever. I could drive around the world. I don't care. I would do it. Could you imagine driving around the world? How funny would that be? You'd be driving underwater sometimes. But I know how some people don't like to drive. I know how some people get like carsick. What is it to some people? — I guess you need to be used to it and some people aren't used to it. But this is something I've always done. My dad took me on long car rides all the time when I was little and we were always going places. Some people are like I can't believe you drove 5 or 6 hours all by yourself. I drove 14 hours by myself! I can be driving and driving and not even realize how long I've gone and it can feel like you can get so tired but then you will get there and you will be like I can't believe we're there. I can't believe what time it is. I can't believe we're here already . . . I love it. Roll the window down. Scream my lungs out . . . And no one can hear me. It's crazy. But I love it.

LORI: I know what you're saying. John has a new car. 755? He's serious about it. He really likes it. He says it gives him freedom. But you can't drive it. He won't let you borrow it. He talks about all the rules. And any time the commercial comes on for his car he gets all red. Points at it. I mean he'll give you a ride, but—you know what I'm saying?

ERIN: There have been so many places that I've been. For vacations. I love to go places for vacations. To travel. You feel so like, free. Freedom. Summer vacations. All over. To be perfectly honest with you, I think my favorite has been the trips to the Islands. You can feel so free.

LORI: Oh I like freedom, too. There have been so many places I've been to, too. So many places. I was on Horn Islands in the Gulf of Mexico on an island in the middle of the ocean. It was so beautiful. They had horses there. Beautiful wild horses there it was so beautiful. There are trees and water. Crystal clear water there. And the sun is warm. I really could have stayed there for a lot longer than I did. I felt like I wasn't spending enough time down there and I wanted to stay longer. But I had to come home. Life wasn't the same after that trip. It was so beautiful. Beautiful island.

ERIN: . . . But there are so many places I want to go. So many places.

JENNIFER: Lori, not riding?

LORI: What.

JENNIFER: You don't like to ride?

LORI: I like riding. What? In the car? I was talking about driving.

JENNIFER: No, for horses. I like horses, too. You said horses. Everyone I know has a horse. I wish I had a horse.

LORI: I'll tell you about horses. Let me tell you about horses. The more you know about horses, the less you know. You can't ever know enough about horses. Horses are something entirely different. First of all—horses are something else— if you want to—horses, well . . .

ERIN: Horses are nice.

LORI: Yeah, horses are nice. Horses—no but I had a horse when
I was 9 years old. Which my dad bought me. And he was
crazy. Crazy. But I loved him. And we would ride all the time
and for the most part he was fine but my dad was always holding the bridle. He was riding with him. And I was on that
horse almost all summer. Because he knew who I was. I could
see it in his eyes. He was a horse. And I loved that horse. But
I knew he knew me and he knew that I knew that he knew
me. You know what I'm saying? He was crazy and he would
throw you. He threw people. And he kicked. But I loved that
horse. And we had to let him go because he was crazy but
I was so sad. So don't tell me about horses and what about
them. Because I know them. They're not just animals.

JENNIFER: Yeah, I agree with you. No I just thought it would be
funny if everyone was riding a horse instead of driving a car.
Like Pony Express.

ERIN: Lori. Do your imitations!

LORI: No.

ERIN: Yes! Come on. Do just one. Do your animals.

LORI: No.

ERIN: Come on! Please! Now?

LORI: No. Not right now.

ERIN: Oh, why?! Please do one. Just one?

JENNIFER: I like them.

LORI: . . . All right.

ERIN: Okay!

JENNIFER: Yes!

LORI: Ready? . . .

*Lori does imitations. The other girls laugh.*

ALL: Ah. That's so funny.

LORI: Hm.

*Pause.*

Oh. Where was I sitting?

*Pause.*

ERIN: Remember that man? Who's that? Remember that man?
Remember that Austin man? Do you know who this person
is? Oh. But I can't remember their name. I'm trying to think
of this person's name. They were around last year and then
they were in Austin for 2 years before that and then they
came here? Do you remember this person? Do you know
who I'm talking about? Do I know? Oh Oh Oh! I almost had
it. Do you know . . . Chris something I want to say. Is it?
Maybe it is. I can't remember. Something like that . . . Well,
they were like here and working I guess and you'd see them
around at different places . . . funny . . . I wish I could
remember . . . I can't remember. Don't you hate that? Oh
I hate that! Oh my God. So much fun we had in those
places. But they were around when we were around and we
used to see them at all different places. But I can't remember their name. Do you know Craig? He's friends with him?
You know who I mean? You know who I'm talking about?
I'm like . . .
JENNIFER: Yeah.
ERIN: Oh my God. Can you believe that?
LORI: Anyway, what about him.
ERIN: He was at Positive Mountain last summer? And then he
was let out for a while and then he went back in again. He's
so messed up. I feel bad for him. He was fine. I never had a
problem with him and all these people were complaining
about him, about his behavior and what they couldn't stand
about how he misbehaved at parties? But I never had a
problem. I feel bad for him? And he's sweet. But they had to
have him back. This time it's for good though. I don't know.
I hope he can cope. You know what I'm saying? I can't
believe I can't remember his name!
JENNIFER: He's good-looking.

ERIN: They talked about how all kinds at church had gotten messed up but they could always handle it and you wouldn't notice that they were having a problem.

JENNIFER: Yeah.

LORI: I know but there it is. I've seen it. See, but I can see those things. You can get into trouble anyway . . . But I know who you're talking about. It's Paul.

ERIN: Paul! Paul! Oh my God! Paul! That's who it is. Lori!

LORI: I know.

ERIN: But Paul got into trouble?

JENNIFER: Yeah.

LORI: No. Paul didn't get into trouble. Paul didn't get into trouble. He was doing fine and then he had to go back. That's all. But Paul didn't get into trouble. Craig got into trouble.

ERIN: Some said it's rock music. I don't know if that's true or not . . .

LORI: What.

ERIN: Paul is into hard rock music.

LORI: No. It's not rock music. It has nothing to do with that.

ERIN: Oh.

LORI: Yeah, well, he is. John told the story of what happened with Paul. It happened at Paul's work. At his work they were all supposed to go white water rafting and John said Paul hates that. But they kind of forced it on him like it was a company thing but the man from the company made it sound like something he had to do: "We want you all to go. It will be good for everyone if everyone goes." And nobody really wanted to go. They were all so glum there. Anyway. So he went and he had a miserable time. Of course. Like he knew he would. And they never really were the same to him from that time on. And he let that bring him down. He got depressed. That's what happened. And John told me it has nothing to do with rock music.

ERIN: Yeah okay.

*Pause.*

I listen to all kinds of music though . . .

*Pause.*

Once, I was walking Ginger in the park and I was listening
to my music. And this really creepy guy is at the park. And
he was like, "Nice dog!" you know, and something gross?
And I had my music on my tape. He came up behind me and
said, "I have a tape player, too. I have a better tape player
than that. Why don't you come listen to your music at my
place. Do you like it? Do you want to do that?" Oh my God.
Ahhh! I couldn't believe it. I like new music. Some people
say all the good music was written before now. I'm like—are
you buying the new music? Are you going to see new music?
Ol' Hot Dog . . . Like those kind of bands. There are so many
good bands.

*Pause.*

LORI: So, did Lee call you?

ERIN: No. He called me again and I like him but I don't like him
when he's drunk and he's always drunk. Because I'm
uncomfortable around him unless I have someone there
with me. To be perfectly honest with you. To be with me
before I begin with him?

JENNIFER: Really?

ERIN: Oh yeah.

LORI: Okay.

ERIN: Yeah. I really do feel that way. I'm tired of dealing with it.
But to be perfectly honest with you, I know I'll see him
again.

LORI: What about Mark?

ERIN: Mark who?

LORI: That man from that money company.

ERIN: Who?

LORI: Didn't he call you?

ERIN: Which Mark?

LORI: Erin. Mark, tall with the suitcase?

ERIN: Oh. Matt!

LORI: Okay, Matt, whatever.

ERIN: Yeah. Matt. He's cute. He called me. We went out. And he's definitely one for the magazines!

JENNIFER: Oh my God.

LORI: Good . . . So, Jennifer. What's going on? Did that one ever call you?

JENNIFER: What? No.

ERIN: You had a good time on that weekend?

JENNIFER: Oh. No. He's funny, though. But I thought you were with John that weekend.

LORI: Yeah . . .

ERIN: You had a weekend together?

LORI: Yeah.

ERIN: Was that Mardi Gras?

LORI: Yeah.

ERIN: How was it?

LORI: John was funny. He likes me to tell him what I'm doing and he watches me do it and then I do it and he says why are you doing it that way? And I tell him that's the way I do it. I say I don't need someone looking over my to tell me what I'm doing and if it's right or wrong. I need—

ERIN: That's all you need.

LORI: Exactly.

JENNIFER: You know who always tells you what to do, exactly.

LORI: He's funny. I don't know. But we always have a good time on Mardi Gras, whether we go or not.

JENNIFER: Mardi Gras was 2 weekends ago.

ERIN: But did you tell him?

LORI: Did I tell him what?

ERIN: What you told me. Or are you just telling me?

LORI: What? I told him.

ERIN: You said that?

LORI: I don't know if that's exact words. I don't care. He knows.

ERIN: Okay.

LORI: No, I'll tell him anything. I know. We can have fun, too.
No, I was at the store and I'm shopping with him and everything is great. See, when John and I are not with other people and when we can talk and he isn't trying to tell me what
to do or not what to do whatever all the time is when things
are great? It's better. It's much better then. We're on the
street. It's a Saturday. People are everywhere. Nobody cares.
I know when he, we could go out on the street and he will be
shopping or whatever something where he is looking for a
jacket or something. And then it's good. Everything is fine.
You know. I like that. That's really nice. But whatever. It's fine.

ERIN: I love it on the weekends.

LORI: You know? With John, there is all this time where it's not
like, "Where is your mom, what's she doin? Is she okay?" You
know, "What time is it?" It's not like that. Because there is time.
And he could have the TV on or whatever. And that's great.
Because his friends are not around and he's really sweet. You
know, we could be on the couch and he's watching a game and
I like that. He's not trying to tell me what to do. It's fine.

ERIN: All the time.

LORI: Exactly.

ERIN: Is he trying to always grab at you and stuff?

LORI: No. I don't care. As long as I don't have to be somewhere.

ERIN: Because I hate that. When they're like, "Oh, please." And
all that. Because I could care less. 'Cause it's like I don't care
if you're Italian. You're not getting anywhere. Not here. Ha ha.

LORI: Ha ha. Please. Yeah.

JENNIFER: You know who you should listen to is LadyBee. She
knows what to do.

ERIN: But I'd love to get away for a weekend.

JENNIFER: Me, too.

*Pause.*

ERIN: . . . Did you guys hear about the sweepstakes? This is cool.
People are in a room and sing their favorite song or do their

favorite trick and these judges from the newspaper come in and pick a winner. Did you hear about this? What would you do? I don't know. I guess you're—well. You're like judged on a lot of different levels. I like thinking about this contest. It could be really funny too. I think the prize is money. Why don't you do your imitation?

LORI: Maybe.

ERIN: Then there's this other contest where they have a photo and you have to guess what the caption would be. You have to decide what they would say. I wonder what you would say? So many contests.

LORI: Maybe I could be champion. Maybe I just need to make more money? Ha ha. I've got so many ideas . . . Now with a television in nearly every home, the possibilities are endless. People will pay for a television show that the public likes. Or finds interesting. I think that's just interesting.

ERIN: Yeah!

JENNIFER: Lori, you mean like Tracy? She made a lot of money.

LORI: Tracy? See, that girl was stupid. See, that girl was stupid. I think. She started. She started working when she was like 16. She was in graphics. But she had to go to school. And schedule her work around it. But she did it. They said she made it work. And then she went to college. Which was good for her. I was happy for her. She made it work. She did it, she had made it with her own business like, 25,000 dollars. Then she went to college and she graduated early and went to work with a T-shirt company. B-Tech something. And they paid her. They paid her good but see she was making T-shirts. Designs for T-shirts. You know? Who wants to make designs for T-shirts. Silk-screening. I mean is that what you want to do? I think she got it backwards. I know I don't want to do it that way. See, it seems to me she peaked way too early. That was the problem. She totally peaked early. For me, I'd rather keep going. I mean you have to have goals. I don't know. I like to manage, manage my time but— differently. I mean to manage it is good but not the way she did it. I'm more into a big-picture approach to it. I am into trying to make all of the projects that I want to do to work out in the right time—work for me, out in time. See, I know when I need to take a break and then I have to take a break from what I'm doing. I have to step back. And I'm always like whoa, I didn't know where I was before. See, then I can take a look at my situation and take a step back from what I'm doing. Because time doesn't mean anything to me. I guess that's what I'm saying.

ERIN: Lori, are you an organizer-type person?

LORI: Why? I mean I can get started okay. But then I like to have the bit parts filled in? Pieces I've forgotten. But I do better if I'm in a familiar situation, doing something that I've done before. Like, my mom was having people over for Christmas and she needed me to clean the guest room, there were all these pictures on her bed and she said, "Clean that bed off." So I did it. And I'd done that room before so I knew how to do it. But I realize you can't know everything. But those are just some examples, like with Jenny—I mean Tracy—she was just—maybe she was just doing too much of one thing in too much of a hurry and she settled for something less than what she could of gotten otherwise. That's all. And this is a separate thing but she also had trouble with love. That's what they said. She couldn't hold on to her man. But I am an organizer-type person. I am an organizer-type because I can get things done if I need to and it helps if I have some experience, too. Ha ha.

ERIN: I think I'm an organizer-type person. To be perfectly honest with you.

LORI: Well, I don't know.

*Pause.*

JENNIFER: I think she may have skills. She might have some skills. You never know.

LORI: Who?

JENNIFER: For Tracy . . .

LORI: Jennifer.

JENNIFER: I'm just saying.

LORI: Jennifer, that's for you. For you that is skillful.

JENNIFER: For her, not for you, maybe. For her. I'm saying.

LORI: Jennifer. I'm not saying that. See, I'm telling—no. But I'm saying—see—if you're doing something and that's all you do—then that's all you know. That's all you see. You would never know something else. But. For me. I have to see more than one thing. See, and that's much better for me. I can get a much better perspective from stepping out of it. I want the best of both worlds. You can't get subjective or whatever. You can't take in everything and expect to survive. I'm not telling you—I know, I'm not—

JENNIFER: No . . . You're not. That's not what I mean.

ERIN: Maybe we should talk about something else.

LORI: No I know I'm not telling you anything you don't know. I know. But you have to take what I say at face value. Otherwise you're doing the thinking for me! And how does that make me feel. You know? So. Don't. Yeah. Of course I am. Of course I am.

JENNIFER: No, that's not it. You don't understand what I'm saying. It's okay.

ERIN: You guys! Why are we talking about Tracy.

LORI: Jennifer. No. Don't get upset. But that is like insulting to me. You're thinking. You're assuming. And that's insulting.

JENNIFER: But I'm telling you that I agree.

ERIN: You guys! Why are we talking about this?

LORI: Okay. Let's talk about something else.

JENNIFER: Okay.

*Pause.*

I hate talking about that anyway.

*Pause.*

. . . Lori. I want to give you this. Let me give you this. I made it myself.

LORI: Jennifer. That you would think of me . . .

*Jennifer gives Lori a necklace.*

JENNIFER: It looks nice on you.

LORI: . . . Oh my God! There's diamond sale at De Beer. Can you believe it? I heard that and I was like: "Ahhhh!" I was like running. Ha ha! They have a lot of stuff.

ERIN: Yeah, they do.

JENNIFER: What are the rings like? Uh-huh.

LORI: Yeah. I like the stuff they have. What? They have rings. Brooches, pendants—all kinds of stuff. They have a Madonna-with-Child that I like.

ERIN: I know. Mother had this stone and they gave her like this whole exam and told her what it was worth on paper. She said, "Let me pay for this!" And they were like, "No, that's okay." You know. "Just think of us next time when you're looking."

LORI: Good.

JENNIFER: I like that place.

*Pause.*

ERIN: You guys, what are we doing? Do you guys want to see a movie? There aren't many good movies out right now. I feel like a lot of the good movies have already come and gone. I like this movie now about the dog and he travels around with a friend who's a cat? It's cute. Then there's this one that looks good . . . People in love with their boss. I don't know. I'm in the mood for a really good movie. You know? That could be really fun since I haven't been in such a long time. We should go. Music-concert movies are fun. And I'll go with the boys to them. That's okay. Every now and then . . . You know. Ha ha. My mom hates me. Ha ha. My mom hates me anyway. Sometimes I think movies are like dreams. You know what I'm saying? They are a place where you can go and be told stories in the dark. I like dreams. I like to analyze them. Who wants to tell me their dream? I would analyze them. Did you know that? Like . . . tell me your dream . . . Jennifer?

JENNIFER: No. I don't want to do that.

LORI: I didn't know you did that. That's wild.

ERIN: Yeah, it was in school for a while. Lori? Tell us a dream and then I'll analyze them.

LORI: I don't know. Ask Jennifer.

ERIN: Jenny, do you want to?

JENNIFER: No way, José.

ERIN: Why not?

JENNIFER: I don't like those kind of things.

ERIN: You guys, it's getting late. Doesn't anyone want me to tell them their dream?

LORI: What?

ERIN: I analyze them. I told you. Tell me your dream.

JENNIFER: I wonder does anyone want to tell their dream. I thought I would analyze them . . .

LORI: Jennifer. No, tell it.

JENNIFER: I don't want to . . .

LORI: Jennifer. Who cares. I have dreams. Who cares if you tell them?

ERIN: So tell us.

LORI: Yeah, tell us.

ERIN: No, Lori. You say your dream.

LORI: Me?

ERIN: Yeah.

LORI: Okay. I had this dream where I was being chased and I couldn't make my arms and legs go. It was weird. Okay. The end. Erin, you have to analyze that.

ERIN: Oh my God. That is so simple. You suffer from stress. Lori, you have too much stress.

LORI: Really?

ERIN: Yeah. That's what it is . . .

LORI: Okay, Jenny. It's your turn.

ERIN: Yeah! Do it.

JENNIFER: I don't think so, you guys, it wouldn't be a good idea.

ERIN: Um . . . Speak.

LORI: Yeah.

JENNIFER: Okay . . .

LORI: See, you're going to do it.

ERIN: Lori, let her tell it . . . Jennifer . . .

JENNIFER: Um . . . I had this dream. I was swimming. There was water. And everyone I knew was there. And I was standing in the middle of this ocean. Which then it turned into this room. And it was sort of like my house but it wasn't. Because then it all changed. And I couldn't make my body do what I wanted it to. Do you know that kind of feeling. It kind of felt like when you're underwater. Or in quicksand. Everything, every move was hard. And I've never felt this way before. It was really freaking me out. And I woke up. But I woke up inside the dream. And it all changed again. Because I thought I was awake. You know. And then I got tired and fell back asleep again. And this time I dreamt I was working for this job. I was running errands for this job. But it was like a test. I was running I was I ran, it was supposed to be this test but I couldn't tell you what it was or what it was supposed to be. It felt very physical. But it was for a job. I had to do this for a job. I knew they were testing me. And I was running and all this in this brick room. The test was like physical, but I said I couldn't do the physical part. It was too hard. I was exhausted and I couldn't do it anymore. I found the test was physical but I couldn't do the physical. Then it was like—well, then we have a mental test for you. And they gave it to me and I looked at it. You know what would you do? I said yes. You know no you know because it's like I had to test and it had to be perfect, actually. And I had to test this with rules that I didn't know what they were. I was to test without knowing what it was

I was supposed to do. And all the questions were like love life questions. Like what would you do if you liked your best friend's boyfriend. Questions like that. That was crazy. But my parents were in this dream and they didn't want me working. They said if I start working they were going to start charging me rent but I said, "If I leave you will rent it out anyway." I didn't know what to do. So I had to quit my job. And I was wondering when I was going to be working again and I wanted to be working again. And I can remember it all really well. But I didn't want to quit my job because all the people in this place were really cool people and they had nice things to say about me and it was nice to hear what they were saying. I liked what the people were saying for a change since they had interesting things to say that weren't part of something they wanted to say to what you thought they wanted to hear. It didn't feel like they were kidding. They weren't being mean. So I didn't plan on liking the people so much but it turned out they had a lot of nice things to say. But I had to quit, so I walked into the hallway and then all the bricks in the room and on the street turned into sky and clouds, and that part was cool. And all there was— like electricity—was burned out and the sky was the only light. You know. And sometimes it was day and that was fine because we had sun, but then it would be night and there would be no light at all. And all the buildings were gone and the sky took over and I remember all this stuff. But I would like to go back to sleep and have that dream again. It was special. That's why I remember it. I remember it all really well . . . I don't know. What kind of dream is that? It's either a really weird dream or just another dream. I don't know which . . .

*Pause.*

ERIN: Oh my God. Jenny.
LORI: Wow.

*Erin and Lori hug Jennifer. Erin sings:*

ERIN:
        I had a dream of you last night
        I woke up thinking about you
        You had me dreaming all last night
        I thought of you
        Do you want me to?

        The way I feel when I'm with you
        Oh, can't you stay with me tonight
        You had me dreaming of the light
        My love it grows
        On my pillows

        I remember you
        I remember you
        You were in my dream
        I remember you

        I remember you
        I remember you
        Up upon the mountaintop
        I remember you

*All sing:*

ALL:
        I remember you
        I remember you
        You were in my dream
        I remember you

        I remember you
        I remember you
        Up upon the mountaintop
        I remember you.

ERIN: Hmmm . . .

LORI: Yeah.

*Doorbell.*

Ohhh!

*Lori goes to get the door. John enters, holding his racing helmet.*

John! Yes! It's you. Oh my God! You guys! . . .

JOHN:

LORI: Oh my God! I'm so happy! These are my friends. This is
Erin.

JOHN: Erin.

LORI: And this is Lisa—I mean Jennifer.

JOHN: How you doin?

LORI: Oh my God! It's so good to see you. Give me a hug.

*They hug.*

JOHN: Yeah.

LORI: Look, you guys. Look who it is . . .

ERIN: John. Did you have a nice drive here from your house?

JOHN: Pretty good. I got here fast enough.

ERIN: That's nice.

JENNIFER:

LORI: So . . . Do you want to see what we bought? Are you ready?

JOHN: Yeah. And.

LORI: Should we go try this stuff on now? Do you girls want to
try this stuff on now?

JENNIFER: I don't really have anything to show though. I think
I'll wait.

LORI: Jenny, you can try my jacket on. Come on, you guys. Let's
try the stuff on. Erin . . .

*The girls exit. John sets his helmet down. Pause.*

JOHN: Meanwhile.

*Jennifer enters in coat.*

What's that?

JENNIFER: This.

JOHN: No. The other.

JENNIFER: This?

JOHN: Yeah.

JENNIFER: I don't know. It's a bowknot. I don't know.

JOHN: Yeah. Did you tie it?

JENNIFER: No.

JOHN: Oh. Okay.

JENNIFER: You are a racer?

JOHN: Yeah.

JENNIFER: What kind of car do you have?

JOHN: Right now?

JENNIFER: Yeah.

JOHN: Open wheel.

JENNIFER: Oh.

JOHN: Hard to drive it, though.

JENNIFER: Oh?

JOHN: Yeah. My reflexes need to be quick. Every second. You know? In the rain? Do you drive?

JENNIFER: You mean for racing?

JOHN: Do you drive a car?

JENNIFER: Yeah. A regular car.

JOHN: A regular car. Okay. Well, that's sort of the same. Regular cars have a lot of the same issues that race cars have. I like the rain personally.

JENNIFER: Oh?

JOHN: Yeah. And I tell a lot people because they don't know that accidents are like driver error. You know? Every three quarters of a second. Constantly decisions, you know? Drivers make mistakes. Cars don't make mistakes. That's true whether it rains or not. But I can't force people to drive safely. People are so rude, right?

JENNIFER: Yeah. *(Smiles)*

JOHN: . . . I'm trying to think of this person's name.

JENNIFER: What.

JOHN: Who you look like . . . Mer. Merle . . . Merlin . . . I don't. Ahhh. You look like that.

JENNIFER: That's nice—Ha ha ha—

LORI *(Offstage)*: John? Where are you. Are you closing your eyes?

*Lori and Erin enter in new outfits.*

JOHN: Huh.

LORI: See . . . What do you think?

JOHN: . . . Good.

LORI: And . . . this.

JOHN: That looks good.

LORI: Look at Erin.

JOHN: You look good.

LORI: "Good." That's all he can say.

JOHN: Where'd the other girl go?

LORI: Where's Jenny. Jenny? Here she is! Wow. Look at her.

JOHN: Oh. Good.

LORI: Okay. That's everybody. We bought this today. Aren't you glad you came over?

JOHN: Yeah.

LORI: Okay. I'll be right back. Come on you guys. We should change.

ERIN: Okay.

*The girls exit. Pause. John exits. Pause. Jennifer enters. Pause. John enters.*

JENNIFER: You forgot the helmet.

JOHN: Yeah . . .

JENNIFER: You and Lori had a weekend together, she said.

JOHN: Yeah.

JENNIFER: That's nice.

JOHN: Yeah, she's—y'know, she is what she is.

JENNIFER: She's nice.

JOHN: Yeah, she's nice! And she's the kind of person who is what I'm talking about. Nobody talks bad about her. I'll kill em. I'll kill anyone who talks bad about her.

JENNIFER: Who talks bad about her?

JOHN: Nobody. Just the guys like to do that sometimes.

JENNIFER: Oh.

JOHN: Yeah and are you smiling?

JENNIFER: I'm not.

JOHN: 'Cause you're like . . .

JENNIFER: That's my face!

JOHN: Oh.

JENNIFER: What!

JOHN: No. I see it. That's your face. Where're you from?

JENNIFER: My family?

JOHN: Yeah, like Scandinavia or something like that I bet.

JENNIFER: . . . I guess . . . My grandma knows.

JOHN: Yeah.

JENNIFER: She knows your mom.

JOHN: She does? Did you ever drive to that place?

JENNIFER: What place.

JOHN: It has the giant statue and the telescope. That's where your people are from, right?

JENNIFER: Yeah, by the observatory or whatever.

JOHN: Yeah.

JENNIFER: Once. Mom used to worry about us going up there, but I think she was worried just so that Grandma would stop worrying about it.

JOHN: I should drive you up there.

JENNIFER: What do you mean?

JOHN: Drive you up there.

JENNIFER: But can you, though?

JOHN: What are you talking about—are you crazy? I would have
    us up there before you could say anything.
JENNIFER: No.
JOHN: But it's fast.
JENNIFER: Okay.
JOHN: Okay, you'll go?
JENNIFER: No. Okay I get it.
JOHN: But what about go?
JENNIFER: To the observatory?
JOHN: Let's do that.
JENNIFER: Right now?
JOHN: Let me do this and then I'll come back.
JENNIFER: Oh my God. Tonight?
JOHN: Yeah. Pick you up.
JENNIFER: Oh.
JOHN: Right?
JENNIFER: Okay . . .
JOHN: You want to, right?
JENNIFER: Um, yeah.
JOHN: You look nice Jennifer. I liked the bow.

*Sings:*

> Give me an answer
> What will it be
> I won't wait forever
> Will you comfort me
>
> I want you so much
> Can't you see
> I want you to touch
> You're heaven to me
>
> You gotta stay with me
> Higher and higher
> I'm reaching higher

Will we chase our dreams
We're coming together
Forever and ever
We'll be

Begin the begin
That's where we met
We were just kids
Always in debt

It's like, "Where can we go?"
It wasn't allowed
You didn't know
What I know now

Will you stay with me
Higher and higher
I'm reaching higher

Will we chase our dreams
We're coming together
Forever and ever
We'll be.

JENNIFER: Yes.
JOHN: Right.

*Erin and Lori enter again.*

LORI: John, aren't you going to take your coat off?
JOHN: No. I'm gonna go.
LORI: No. So soon?
JOHN: Yeah. I got this to do. We're gonna run tonight.
LORI: What?! Why didn't you tell me? Where? We'll go see it.
JOHN: No. The crew's gonna run tonight. We're not opening up.
    It's just practice.

LORI: But can't we come?
JOHN: No, It's just practice.
LORI: Oh, well, you can stay for a little longer.
JOHN: No. I gotta go. My car's outside.
LORI: What? Let me see it! Which one? The new one? John!
JOHN: No, it's out there, the regular one . . . Bye.
LORI: Oh. Wait. Don't I get.
JOHN: Yeah, you got it.

*They kiss.*

LORI: Bye, Johnny.
JOHN: Bye.

*John exits.*

JENNIFER: Bye.
LORI: Oh my God . . . You guys! Can you believe him. He's so
    funny. I love that jacket on him.

*Pause.*

Well, that's enough activity for me. Good night. *(Exits)*
ERIN: Good night. Well, Jennifer? Are you going to come to bed?
JENNIFER: No. I think I'll stay up a little longer.
ERIN: Okay. I'll see you in the morning. Don't have any more
    crazy dreams, okay? *(Exits)*
JENNIFER: Ha ha.

*Pause. John enters.*

Hi.
JOHN: Shhh . . . they'll hear you. C'mon. Over here . . . That's
    nice. Thank you. Okay, see? Yeah
JENNIFER: My mom isn't into the idea of premarital sex too
    much these days.

JOHN: That's okay.

JENNIFER: Well, I don't know . . .

JOHN: See how it goes. Come on, it's fun. See?

*They kiss. Jennifer sings.*

JENNIFER:
> Will I survive
> Will I survive
> I'm sad and low
> I'm sad and low
>
> I stand frozen now
> But I got here somehow
> If you could help me out
> 'Cause I can't help myself
>
> People on the street
> But our eyes they don't meet
> I'm glad their eyes don't see
> I'm glad they don't see me
>
> Take a look at me
> Tell me what you see
> I am standing here
> And I cannot break free
>
> So the story goes
> Will I be alone
> I'm sad and low
> Those people don't know
> So the story goes
>
> Will I survive?

JOHN: See. I told you! We better get back. Okay. Bye . . .

JENNIFER: John . . .
JOHN: Shhh.

*He kisses her. Lori enters.*

LORI: John, is that you? . . . What's going on?
JOHN: Ohh!
JENNIFER: Where have you been?
LORI: Jennifer, what are you talking about?
JENNIFER: What?
LORI: John, what is going on?
JOHN: Nothing. We were just talking.
LORI: What is happening here?
JOHN: What am I doing?
LORI: John, get out.
JOHN: No way.
LORI: Get out, now.
JOHN: I'm trying to tell you something.
LORI: John. Go away.
JOHN: Huh. I was talking to her. What about her?
LORI: Get out.

*John exits.*

JENNIFER: John!
LORI *(To Jennifer)*: Okay for you girl.
JENNIFER: Lori, he was just here.

*Erin enters.*

ERIN: What's going on?
LORI: I caught her messing around with John.
ERIN: Which John?
LORI: My John.
ERIN: Oh my goodness. You're joking. Jenny?
LORI: I'm not kidding.

ERIN: Really?

LORI: Really.

ERIN: When?!

LORI: Erin. Stop. Just now.

ERIN: Well, okay . . .

JENNIFER: Well.

LORI: Oh. Are you going to talk now?

ERIN: Oh. Okay. What are you going to do, you guys?

LORI: I'm going to kill this girl.

JENNIFER: I'm going to kill this girl.

ERIN: Come on you guys. Let's calm down. You know what I'm
saying? Jenny. Lori. Why don't you let Jenny explain what
happened . . .

LORI: I saw what happened. I'm not in the mood.

JENNIFER: I'm not in the mood.

ERIN: Don't be crazy. You guys, everybody settle down.
Jennifer—

LORI: Erin, shut up, stop playing around . . .

ERIN: Tell us, Jennifer.

JENNIFER: I was to go with John.

LORI: What do you mean, "go with John."

JENNIFER: When you were changing with Erin, John asked me
to go with him.

LORI: Go with him where?

JENNIFER: Well, go with him to the telescope, but go with him
go with him.

LORI: What's she talking about Erin?

ERIN: What are you talking about? John never asked you to go
with him.

JENNIFER: That's what he said.

LORI: Get out, Erin . . .

ERIN: Lori?

LORI: Get out of here!

ERIN: What? Lori—

LORI: Get out of here! I'm talking to Jennifer!

ERIN: Lori, what are you talking about? I didn't do anything.

*Lori pushes Erin. She falls.*

LORI: Get the hell out of here! Now!
ERIN: Oh my God!

*Lori goes for Erin. Erin runs. Lori throws Jennifer to the floor.*

JENNIFER: Ahhh!!!
ERIN: What are you doing?!

*Lori sits on Jennifer's chest.*

Oh my God, you're hurting her. Lori, get off! It reminds me of a thing that happened to me, Lori. And all I can say is, it was a moment of terrible sadness but it passes! Lori! Wait, Lori—wait . . . You're my friend. You're my best friend, Lori. I love you. There's so much to say. You don't know. You don't know what you're doing. Because now I think about everything and how it might have been different. I can't believe what's happening. But I look at you now and I can't believe how long it's been and it doesn't seem right. I don't care if it's right or not. But what about to try and make it different? I don't know. It's too painful for me, otherwise. This isn't right. Why can't we all get along.

*Sings:*

> Don't walk away now
> Don't leave me alone
> Things aren't the same now
> You never would have known
>
> You gotta take chances
> And get to me somehow
> Take the time romance it
> Say my name out loud

> Somehow
> Somehow
> Let me tell you
>
> You have to follow your heart
> Let me know
> So I can know who you are
> Let it show

*Lori sings with Erin:*

ERIN AND LORI:
> You have to follow your heart
> Let me know
> So I can know who you are
> Let it show.

*The phone rings.*

ERIN: Hello?

LORI: Who is it?

ERIN: No, she's busy right now. Who's this? . . . Yes . . . Oh! . . .
Oh, no . . . Yes. Oh no. Oh my God. He did? Oh . . . Oh no . . .
Okay . . . Yes . . . Okay . . . Okay . . . Mm-hmm . . . Okay . . . Oh
. . . I know . . . Oh no. Well . . . I know . . . All right. Bye . . .

LORI: What is it?

ERIN: Oh my God. That was John's mom. The sheriff just called
her. John was killed in an accident.

LORI:

ERIN: Lori, please.

LORI: . . . Mm-hmm.

ERIN: Lori. I have something to tell you.

LORI: Okay.

ERIN: . . . John was killed in an accident.

LORI: What?

ERIN: He was killed in his car. Apparently, he was very upset. Oh
my God. This isn't right . . .

LORI: Oh my God.
JENNIFER: Oh my God.

*Pause.*

LORI: You guys. I guess this is it.

*Sings:*

> You know the way home
> But you cannot go there
> And I see but I can't believe
> How I'll never be the same again
>
> Oh how I love you
> I can't be the same without you
> Oh how I love you
> I can't live without your love

*Jennifer and Erin sing with Lori:*

ALL:

> Come home, you never know
> It's never the same, I told you so
> And you'll see, what this place'll be
> I can't believe how it's changed me
>
> You know the way home
> But you cannot go there
> And I see but I can't believe
> How I'll never be the same again
>
> Oh how I love you
> I can't be the same without you
> Oh how I want you
> I can't live without your love
> Oh how I need you
> I can't live without your love.

# CAVEMAN

*Caveman* was workshopped in December 1999 at Soho Rep in New York City. Direction by the author. Set and costumes by Stephanie Nelson. Lights by Eric Dyer. Original cast:

| | |
|---|---|
| W | Tory Vazquez |
| C | Tony Torn |
| A | Jim Fletcher |

In April 2001 it premiered at Soho Rep. Change in cast:

| | |
|---|---|
| C | Lakpa Bhutia |

Musicians:

Greg Hirte (Violin)
Bryan Kelly (Bass)
Scott Sherratt (Guitar)

*W enters, takes off coat, crosses to kitchen, microwaves dinner.*
  *She sings:*

w:
  Baby
  I love you
  Baby
  I'll find you

  Baby, I'll find you
  Baby, yes I will
  Baby, I love you
  Yes, I do
  Let it be true
  I love you

  Baby
  I love you
  Baby
  Yes, I do

  Baby can you tell me
  I love you
  Baby can you tell me
  I'll find you.

 Where have you been?

c *(Waves her off)*: That man is coming over.

w: What man?

c: From the warehouse. Angelo.

*Pause.*

w: So I had an inneresting conversation today.

c: Who.

w: Well, Jackie said they knew of a group in San Antonio that
will help and so I said let's go. I said we'd all go to San
Antonio instead of Driscoll. Great! He said all these people
will go. But now since Rickie doesn't want to go it's 17 dollars more a day. And now Jackie said it's getting too expen-
sive and I'm saying don't go if all you're going to do is complain. These people, Jackie, Rickie, are complaining to me
as if I planned this to happen. I didn't plan for this to happen. I say you can help or not. It's up to you. But you know
if we're not going to stick together then what's the point? We
might as well not do it.

c: So what are you going to do?

w: I'm not gonna tell them. I'm just going to pay their 17 dollars.

c: Don't pay it.

w: Well, I want to go.

c: I know.

*Pause.*

w: I went with Cheryl to Sam's and there were so many people
out. It was really making me crazy . . . I had so much
I wanted to get. I didn't end up getting anything. I don't like
going over there. It's so crowded. Cheryl bought craft sticks
and buttons and things. I thought she had a cute idea. She's
going to make a mouse out of a sock and put it in a box for
Father's Day. She has good ideas. Cheryl is a real inspira-
tion. She can make anything. I look at her and I think: I can
do that. And she said she doesn't worry about making mis-

takes. She said that a lot of times mistakes can be beautiful. So don't throw it away until you have given it a fair chance! That's what she said . . . I don't know what to say about that . . . But she dropped me off. I had to wait in the rain. There was no bus. There was no shuttle. I had to take TaxiService. You know? And then, I come home to this place and it looks like a simple disaster!

*Pause.*

What do you think about that?

*Pause.*

But Cheryl said Paulie wasn't going to be needing the car next weekend . . . I thought that might be an idea . . . Do you want me to call Paulie to get the car, then?

c: No. What for?

w: To get the car.

c: Car for what, woman?

w: To go to San Antonio.

*C sits.*

c: Oh, I don't care about that. I'll tell you what. I said no. I don't want to go.

w: Why not?

c: I'm tired. Look at me.

w: It won't take that long—you could go to the track.

c: I don't like it! It brings me down.

w: We could go and be back.

c: I don't like it! If you want to talk about it, tell them! I don't like talking about it

w: Well! Fine! I'll go by myself!

c: Go! I don't want to hear about it

w: Okay, then! I'll go by myself! *(She cries)*

*C gets up and stops her from crying, sits again.*
*W sings:*

Dry your eyes
Daylight watch o'er me
And paradise
Is there and waits for me

Don't shed a tear
I'm where I want to be
I feel you near
I cry myself to sleep
In the night
Dry your eyes
I heave a sigh

*C sings with W:*

W AND C:
When daylight goes by
I cry myself to sleep
By the night
I'm where I want to be
Day into night
Daylight lies
Cries next to night . . .

C: Okay.

*W crosses to kitchen. Knock.*

Come in.
A: I'm coming over.
C: I know it's you
A: Where should I sit? By the table?
C: In the chair is good.

A: Yeah . . .

W: What's that smell? It smells like garbage.

C: Don't worry about it.

W: Oh hello.

A: You know I wanted to ask you. You had all your starter pieces
   chosen for you, right?

*W brings plates.*

C: Eat now.

A: Oh yeah. Great . . .

*They eat in silence.*

C: Were you on the floor today?

A: Yeah.

C: Okay. Lot of people didn't show up, no?

A: Huh?

C: Don't you think?

A: Why?

C: 'Cause it's Friday?

A: I don't know. Yeah.

*Pause.*

C: Did you see that girl?

A: Yeah.

C: That one with the ass.

A: Yeah.

C: Ohh . . .

A: What.

C: I want to fuck that girl.

A: Yeah. *(Smiles)*

C: Huh? *(Smiles)* Right? Who is she?

A: I don't know.

C: She's nice, though, right?

A: Yeah . . .

C: Don't you think?

A: Yeah.

C: What's her name?

A: I'm not sure.

C: Why don't you find out who she is?

A: Why me?

C: Don't you want to know?

A: You do.

C: I know. But you work with her. You know?

A: Yeah.

C: Yeah. You find out.

A: Okay, guy.

C: Don't you think she's nice?

A: Yeah.

C: Huh?

A: Yeah. She's okay.

C: She comes up to you and talks in your face. With the eyes . . .

A: Yeah.

C: I wonder what she sees.

A: . . . I think I see what you mean. I mean I never thought about
   it, but now I see. I agree with you . . .

C: Open. Look. Listen . . .

A: Yeah. I agree. I agree with you.

C: Beautiful. So beautiful . . . What about you? What do you like?

*W crosses to them.*

W: Maybe later we can get that car then like I said and go for a
   ride.

C: Maybe, is right.

A: Ride. Who wants a ride?

W: I do.

C: She wants to go for a ride.

A: Where to?

W: Yeah. No. You don't have to go.

c: It's for her son.

w: It's his son, too.

a *(To W)*: I had no idea you had a son.

c: Yeah well, maybe she does, maybe she doesn't.

a: Oh yeah? I have a car.

w: You do?

c: You don't have a car.

a: Yeah.

c: What kind is it?

a: It's an M car.

c: That's not a car.

a: Well, I think it is.

w: It's not a big deal. He doesn't have a car. But we have to borrow rides. He expects me to do it. I don't mind. We'll find a
way. I'm the kind of person, I wake up and I say, "What can
we do today?" Projects. There are all these projects that I'm
into. You know? You can't be afraid to try something new.
Hundreds of things you can do with things lying around the
house.

c: What is this? Toastmistress?

a: I'm just listening.

c: You're just like your mother.

w: I am like my mother.

c: All right! I'm sure he's real innerested in that!

a: She's just having a conversation with me. *(To W)* No, you don't
look like you had a son.

c: But she did.

a: Yeah, I got it.

*W crosses to kitchen.*

c: She gets upset. She can't handle it by herself.

a: What kind of accent is that?

c: She doesn't have an accent . . .

a: . . . This your place?

c: You bet.

A: All yours?

c: Yeah.

A: You don't pay rent?

c: No I do not.

A: Well, well . . .

A:

c: What's on your mind, Angelo?

A: Anthony.

c: Yeah.

A: Yeah. Okay. Let's get to business.

c: What's going on down on the floor?

A: Yeah.

c: . . . Go.

A: People are confused.

c: About what?

A: Well, it all comes down to whose system, whose model you want to use: the one that we use now is if you worked on their system, I mean for their system, what's to stop me from, okay, it's like—what is the goal from our side? You know what I'm saying? I could work for you and we'd be good, we could make it happen, right? And that's fine, and we'd be fine, you know? But what if you and I were to, come to see what would come of this some kind of thing and where we didn't have to show the differences. You know? What would they say?

c: Yeah . . .

A: We could give a statement or whatever that shows that they're the same?

c: No.

A: Why not.

c: Because they're not the same.

A: Then we got a problem here, like I said. Because we can't agree on which system to use. On one hand you have the old way which is more traditional and established . . . which most everybody knows, but it's really for old people—and then you have the new way that I like better because the young people feel better about it—people who are new are looking at the old model and saying, "What is this?" So basically it is about the old way versus the new way. And I don't care really, but we need to decide—and I'm like well let's decide.

c: How long have you worked here?

a: How long . . . 9 months.

c: 9 months. That's it? You know how long I have worked here?

a: I don't know. I got here, and you were here.

c: I'm here for 13 years, son. *(Smiles)*

a: Yeah. Well, like I'm saying. I have worked in it for over 9 months and have been involved in pretty major projects. I saw a lot of pride from people. And different people have different ways of dealing with it.

c: Whoa whoa whoa. Pride? You talk about pride. That's funny to me, because you don't know what pride is. How long have you been working here? 9 months. You know? What time did you get up this morning? What time did you get home? See? That's pride, son. I have worked in these places, and I have seen this place go from the worst to a little bit better. Okay? I know about pride. Yeah, when you have worked for 13 years, then you can talk about pride. You understand?

a: Yeah. Well, I don't know.

c: Exactly. You don't know.

a: Yeah, well, like I said. I don't know . . .

c: Back up, son . . . Pride. Pride goes back. 1928. Before that, the Middle Ages. You can trace it. There have been transitions but it's still the same. Delivering frozen foods: taco, chicken, hot bagels, pizza, whatever. Delivering to: IFH, Robert E. Lee, Wolf . . . Le Fleur Foods. Dos Amigos, IGA, Solo. Texas, Georgia, Oklahoma, North Carolina, Virginia. Store-brand and controlled-brand environments. 600 stores. 28,000 items. —Wholesale food. Tobacco, alcohol. Wide distribution. I'll tell you what.

a: Well, like I said. I don't care. I'm just like well, let's pick a system and stick with it. You know, I don't care, new, old, it doesn't matter. Let's just pick one.

C: We *have* a system. Let me explain to you. I worked in the warehouse and they were using the younger people's system and it was a newer system. Their way is all about speed and that's not right. You know? And after that I swore I would never do it their way again. I'll tell you what.

A: But that's their system, though with the starter pieces . . .

C: Well, it's a cold reality, son. But it's not a big deal. Cheer up. *(Smiles)* . . . Great things come at a price. There's nothing you can do. It might be depressing for you. But it's a cold reality and there's nothing you can do, son.

*Pause.*

A: Yeah, but you know what? . . . I would never have worked under their system. The old way.

C: That's different from what you just said . . .

A: Yeah, well . . .

C: Yeah? Why not?

A: Because.

C: Why not?

A: No. I won't do it, actually. I'll never do it . . . I wouldn't do it.

C: Why not?

A: Well I have my reasons.

C: What are they?

*Pause.*

A: 'Cause. It gives me a headache sometimes! What about the new system. I don't see what's wrong with it. People are talking about the new system. There's a manual on it that's out now . . . What do you think about it, buddy?

C: Well, I will make the final decision on this. Yes. I will make the final decision on this. And what I decide you will have to accept. So I'm not just thinking about you, but you, me, and everyone else here . . . so yeah. And everyone else seems to be fine with the old way. That's my experience . . .

A: But I'm telling you what everyone else thinks and they think the old way stinks.

C: Yeah, that's not my experience.

A: Everybody who I talk to says it doesn't work.

C: Well, that's not my experience.

A: Aww! You don't know! Your experience. You don't know! You don't know the people! Why don't you try it. Just try it and see what the people think!

C: No, son!

A: Son?!

C: It won't work!

A: Come on!

C: It doesn't work.

*W brings beer.*

W: You're yelling! Why don't you sit down . . .

A: We'll see.

C: Okay. You don't tell me which system is best. I tell you. Really.

A: Okay, guy. No, I got it.

*Pause.*

I'm looking at your body. You got a funny body.

C: Oh?

A: Yeah. Look at it . . . Let me see something . . . Okay . . . This is your chest, right? . . .

C: What about you? Look at you.

A: What.

C: You look like Neandrathal.

A: Who's that?

C: You're big. No question.

A: I know.

C: Right? You weren't always this big . . .

A: Yeah!

C: . . . How did you get so big?

A: Yeah you know what it is?

C: Yeah.

A: You know what it is?

C: Yeah.

A: Phosphogates.

C: What are they?

A: Phosphogates. Yeh. Yeah. Phosphogates. That's what it is. But you gotta eat.

C: Yeah?

A: Yeah. Phosphogates.

C: Okay, I got it.

*Pause.*

I'll tell you what.

A: Yeah.

C: Those can make you crazy.

A: No no no no. Listen.

C: Be careful, son.

A: They don't make you crazy. What I'm talking about is a catalyst. It's all catalytic converters. What you're talking about? Those aren't steroids. Cortisol. Cortisone. Prednisone. Those aren't—they're converters—for the anabolic. Picture rings. Just picture rings. And these rings form with other rings and you get the picture. Rings. Steroids just affect the body size. You might be thinking about what are called corticosteroids. That's different . . . I can't remember his name. English bloke? —Had chickens. And one was on the hormone. And one wasn't. What happens? You know what happens? The chicken have a red hat on their head, right? For the chicken whom was not on the hormone was really small. Had this LITTLE small thing—

C: A crown?

A: Yes! A crown. Little thing crown. And the other one?

C: Was big . . .

A: Exactly. Nice big one.

c: All right.

a: But I also work out. The chickens weren't working out, exactly. You gotta work out. So? That's all. You know. If you keep taking them, and keep taking them, then maybe you'd go crazy. But that's true with most things. That's true with everything! But you're not going to go crazy. They're not going to make you crazy. I mean they could make you crazy. But they're not going to make you crazy.

c: Yeah.

*Pause.*

w: He doesn't go in for those programs.

*Pause.*

a: All right?

c: All right. That's inneresting.

a: But are you interested? You said you were interested but a lot of times people say they're interested when they're not really interested.

c: No. It's inneresting.

a: You want me to write it down?

c: Yeah.

a: Okay.

*W gets a pencil. A writes it all down.*

*(To C)* You want a cigarette?

c: Yeah.

*W gets matches, lights it.*

a: Oh, I like that!

*They smoke. Pause.*

Do you think you could take me?

c: Uhn?
a: I bet I can take you.
c: Depends. That depends, son.
a: Yeah. I bet.

*W brings an ashtray. She sings:*

w:

    When I was young and the days growing up
    When it's so cold that your face freezes up
    Not like today where it can't even snow
    But in those days it was a hundred below

    Z-104 was the frequency mode
    I can remember listening all alone
    Static and cold, the driveway is blocked
    The sun's going down and the temp'rature drops

    I'll be here when you are gone
    I'll live on

    I, will get to a place
    Where I, can see my face

    Yeah I, look in the mirror
    But my, face won't appear

    Now I'm a ghost here and Mexicans come
    They come to my house and I feel over-run
    They come to my town and expect to be fed
    But I will protect those who are living and dead

    I'll be here when you are gone
    I'll live on

    I, will get to a place
    Where I, can see my face

Yeah I, look in the mirror
But my, face won't appear

I, can't be a ghost
When I, am a secret to most!

A: She's got a nice body. You know it?
C: Yeah. I like it.
A: I bet you do.
C: Yes . . .
A: Nice. What about her? What's with her?
C: She's with me.

*Pause.*

A: How'd that happen?
C: Uhn?
A: What's she doing with you?
C: What.
A: How come?
C: She's with me.
A: She looks good. I don't know . . .
C: Yeah. Like I said. She's mine.
A: I don't know . . . Why don't I just take her?
C: Ha ha. I don't think so.
A: Right. You're right.
C: I think you're joking . . .
A: Probably. I wouldn't want her that way. I'm not like that.
C: Uhn.
A: Unless she wanted me.
C: Oh yeah.
A: Then I'd take her.

*Pause. W brings refills.*

I'm telling you. She does it all for you, don't you, hush-puppet.
Answer me.

w: Excuse me, I'm busy right now doing things while you're sitting here, but you aren't going to call me by my name, are
   you?
a: I don't know your name!
w: That's all right.
a: . . . Tell me your name!

*W crosses to kitchen.*

Tell it! . . . Ha ha.

*A stands up. Pause. W crosses to C.*

c: What are you doing?
a: I'm looking for the bathroom.
c: Take a right.
a: Yeah.
c: Right there.
a:
c: Right there!
a: Right . . . ?
c: Stupid!
a: What?
c: Stupid!
a: Hey. No.

*C smiles.*

Tell me where it is.
c: Go right!
a: I'm warning you, guy.
w: Say. Don't ever do that to me again.
c: What did I do?
w: Don't ever let me say that again.
c: What happened?

w: I didn't know he was here. I would never had said it stunk in here if I knew he was here. That's embarrassing. You tell me when we have visitors.

c: Aww . . . He doesn't know.

w: I'm not kidding. Don't ever do that to me again.

c: Hey. He—hey. He's lost. Show him where the bathroom is.

w: Hello.

A:

w: Did you find it?

A:

w: Anthony, you said you have a car.

A: You let your hair down.

w: Well, I like it like this.

A: I like it, too.

w: Thank you.

A: Mm.

w: Do you ever borrow your car?

A: Yeah. What for?

w: Well, we—

A: I use it though. For work.

w: Do you work every day?

A: Yeah.

w: Isn't there a day where you get to goof off?

A: Sunday. You want to borrow it?

w: Well, I want to, yes. It's important . . . I had photos of the memories. And I found all these maps. And the maps had all this blue and green on it. So I put together a vacation showcase with maps and photos. It's pretty nice. I took all the ticket stubs of places we went together. Now I'm hoping to retrace my steps. I look at the maps and I feel better. It keeps me going. I need to get out more. I see all the places I haven't checked, and I need to get out more. I can find out more. But there's so much to do . . . I don't know. I've written all these letters to my friends. I love to do it! They are all very supportive. They offer their suggestions. It's fun! In a lot of ways, it feels like a second chance.

A: Okay. I believe you.

w: Thank you.

A: No. If you say so. I believe you.

w: He's really bad with people. He doesn't talk to anybody. *(C stands)* So I end up talking to everybody and explaining and telling how he isn't a bad person. I mean, it's not really about whose fault it is. It doesn't matter. It's not about that. It's not about fault. It doesn't matter.

A: It doesn't matter to me.

w: Right, that's how I feel! But I'm a very passionate person.

*Pause.*

A: Yeah, you are. Did you notice something?

w: What?

A: Down there.

w: What.

A: You're showing a bit of leg there.

w: Anthony, don't.

A: Did you notice!

w: Yes, I noticed.

*They kiss. Pause. W crosses to C.*

A: (Yes.)

*A sings:*

> Number 1
> Have fun
> On Sunday
> You can play

> Number 2
> It's work, too
> Work hard
> Get large

My deal, this is for real
You're worried
It doesn't bother me

Number 3
Be with me
Take my hand
Understand

Okay, now it's number 4
Has this ever happened before?
See the colors see the shapes
See the people make mistakes

The calendar and my clock count
But I can do it by myself
Look up in the sky is blue
See the clouds pass by you, too

It's my deal, this is for real
You're worried
It doesn't bother me

Number 5
Stay alive
Be with me
Number 3.

c: Listen. You want a girl? What kind of girl do you like?
a: Don't worry about me, guy.
c: No, maybe I'll come up with something.
a: No, you don't know what I'm talking about.
c: Sure. That's what I'm tellin you.
a: No, I like . . . I don't know.
c: You like tits. Right?
a: I like tits. I like nice tits.

C: What about ass?

A: What about it?

C: Tell me.

A: Ass yeah. Round.

C: Like a bubble. Ass. I know. With the shoulders. I know.

A: Yeah.

C: You like fat?

A: They're okay. Skinny too.

C: You like black girls?

A: Black? I don't know.

C: How about yellow?

A: It's okay. Yellow.

C: So all kinds, then. Let me think about it. Yeah. You can find
   something.

A: No I know. I've seen it.

C: Right? I've seen it, too.

A: But I mean in real life?

C: What?

A: In reality.

C: I don't know what you mean.

A: Look . . . Do you see her in real life?

C: Hhhhh.

A: In real life or in magazines?

C: I don't know what you mean.

A: You like the magazines?

C: Like porn? Pornos?

A: Yeah. Is it like that?

C: Yeah . . . Is that what it's like?

A: In magazines?

C: Yeah . . .

A: Is she like that? Is that what it's like?

C: Yeah . . .

A: Yeah. That's all right and everything. But I know what it all
   really looks like. I've seen it for real. It's not like the magazines. I know what it looks like. I've seen it. I know what she
   looks like.

c: Is it beautiful?

a: Yes. It is. It is right. It's all right.

c: It is beautiful.

a: Yeah!

c: Yes. I know what you mean.

a: I want it, too. I want it so bad. Do you know?

c: Yes! Yes! Beautiful!

a: Ha ha ha!

c: Ha ha!

*Pause.*

a: . . . I like her.

*Pause.*

I'm telling you.

w: What the hell are you talking about? Don't you see me standing here?

c: Don't worry about it.

*Pause.*

w: He gambles.

c: Hey. Woman!

w: No, it's not like nobody knows about it. In fact, everyone
   knows about it. He's famous for it. He's a gambler. It's not a
   bad thing. You can be like all those people who say he isn't
   worth anything because he's a gambler and he made bad
   bets but I don't think that's fair. Do you? People don't think
   about how he's very well known here plus when you're
   famous like that, it helps everybody because now we're on
   the map but they won't appreciate it until he's gone. It
   swings you know, for him. He gambles. And that's okay . . .
   But there isn't any money left over for extras like protein
   powder and magazines or gasoline.

c: Hey. What are you saying?

w: What.

c: That sounds like double-talk, to me.

w: I don't think it is.

c: Goddamn it, woman!! Look around. It's not just me here.

w *(To C)*: Here.

*Pause. She hands C a piece of paper.*

c: What's going on? What's with this paper. Where'd you get this paper?

w: I want you to make a few phone calls. I want to talk to some people who might lend us a car to go to San Antonio.

a: Well, now . . . San Antonio! That sounds nice!

w: Yes . . .

a: Hey, are we all going to San Antonio?

c: No.

a: Aww!!!

c: Why don't you settle down.

a: Settle down?! This should be more like a party. Can you imagine if this was a party? I would tell jokes and you would eat snacks. And she could sit on my lap. Now come on over here and sit on my lap.

c: That's not the way . . . Hey!

a: What about that ride? Should we go?

c: We should not, boy.

*A grabs W's wrist. Pause.*

a: Look at how small you are. You have such little wrists. Look.

w: Don't.

a: Let me see. *(Stands)* I can put my hands around your waist. I can put my hands around her waist . . . Ha ha . . . How come you're so small? How come she's so small? *(He holds her)*

c: I guess some people are bigger than others, lummox.

A: Yeah!

*A kisses W. C intervenes, A pushes C, a scuffle. A picks up W.*

w: Stop.
c: Put her down!
A: Ohh!
w: Put me down!
c: Hey!
A: Maybe you need to listen to me.
c: What.
A: I have what she wants. *(To W)* I have what you want. You
   know I have it.
c: Don't.
A *(To W)*: You wanna see something?
c: I'm talking to you.
A: No you wouldn't understand.
c: You're crazy.
A: Maybe I need to make you understand.
c: Maybe you do . . .
A: Maybe I do . . .
w: It's okay. I don't need to go.
A: But you could go if you wanted to. *(To C)* It's your move . . .
c: . . . Come on then.

*They fight.*

Wait wait wait. Noo!
w: Stop!
A: Ahhh!

*A and W scream.*

Please . . . please. Go with me. I'll help you. I like to help.
I like it. Go with me and I'll help you. I'll help you find your
son. I know lots of people who will help us. Please. Listen

to me. I want you. I want you. I want you to go with me.
Please go with me!

w: Oh, Anthony, this is it. Try to understand. Come, come,
Anthony. I can't stop. I can't take a breath. I have to make
something happen. I need to step outside and get around to
different places. I know. I've seen it. I can make something
happen. You know? It feels like my childhood all over again,
but this time, I'm smarter, SLOWER, and a whole lot more
ready. There are so many people in this world. So many
faces. All these faces don't mean anything to me unless
I find him. Some things are so beautiful. But there isn't anything.

*C sings:*

c:

    I can't tell you
    How I feel for you
    But I feel for you
    I love you, too

    Yes, I do
    I love you
    I mean it, too
    Please love me, too

    Please believe, it's hard for me
    Please believe really, so hard for me

    I'm not trying to keep you down
    You could leave, but you wouldn't be around

    I love you
    Yes, I do
    I mean it, too
    I love you

> I can't tell you
> How I feel for you
> But I feel for you
> I love you, too

> I love you
> Yes I do
> I love you
> Please love me, too.

*C hugs W.*

Shh. Shhh. It's okay. Okay. I love you. It's okay.
w: I love you, too.

*Sings:*

> Oh, my dears, I'm tired now, I'm tired now
> No more beer, or cigarettes
> I'll get by somehow

> Rest your head, my babe
> Sweet dreams, my babe
> Rest your head, my babe
> Sweet dreams, my babe

> Now my breath, is telling me, it's cold again
> Here it comes, my feet are numb
> I feel it begin

*C and A sing:*

C AND A:
> Sweet dreams, my babe
> Rest your head, my babe
> Sweet dreams, my babe.

# BOXING 2000

*Boxing 2000* premiered in September 2000 at the Present Company Theatorium in New York City. Direction by the author. Set and costumes by Stephanie Nelson. Lights by Eric Dyer. Original cast:

| | |
|---|---|
| JO-JO | Gary Wilmes |
| PROMOTER | Chris Sullivan |
| FREDDIE | Robert Torres |
| MARISSA | Gladys Perez |
| OL' KID HANSEN | Jim Fletcher |
| REFEREE | Lakpa Bhutia |
| AFLECK | Alex Ruiz |
| CORNER | Candido "Pito" Rivera |
| FATHER | Benjamin Tejeda |

An earlier version was presented in December 1999 at the Experimental Theater Wing, New York University, in New York City.

# 1

*Jo-Jo, Fred and the Promoter are talking.*

JO-JO: Smell this . . .
FRED: What's that.
JO-JO: Terrible, right?
FRED: Yeah.
JO-JO: Smells like licorice, right?
FRED: What is that?
JO-JO: It's for barf.
FRED: Oh yeah, exactly.

   *Pause.*

JO-JO: Fred, did you see that fight last night?
FRED: The first round?
JO-JO: The whole thing.
FRED: That was the whole thing.
JO-JO: No. Which fight?
FRED: The first one.
JO-JO: No. Bro, I'm talkin about the second one.
FRED: Okay.
JO-JO: The second fight, was better, even. The first round?
FRED:
JO-JO: The guy was like—bowh! *(Swings at Fred)*

*Jo-Jo laughs. He pushes Fred.*

FRED: Yeah . . .

JO-JO: What's his name?

FRED: I don't know.

JO-JO: Jamie . . . Jamie . . . I tried callin Dad last night to watch it.

FRED: Okay.

JO-JO: Yesterday was his birthday . . .

FRED: Yeah, I know.

JO-JO: I wonder what to get Dad for his birthday. Shirt . . . pants . . . suit . . .

FRED: You should get him a suit.

JO-JO: I don't know.

FRED: You should get him a suit.

JO-JO: I don't know. He just got a suit. He just got 3 new suits.

FRED: I don't know.

JO-JO: Yeah. He just got a suit. I don't know what to get him. I know all these people already got him stuff and I can't think of anything to get him . . . My kids already got him stuff. Even they already know what they're gonna get him. Deeana knows, even. Everybody knows.

FRED: What are your kids get him?

JO-JO: I don't know. They wouldn't tell me. Now I'm like where I don't know what they got; I'm afraid what they got is what I'm gonna get. You know?

FRED: Whaddya wanna get him?

JO-JO: I don't know what I wanna get him. I don't know what I wanna get him.

FRED: I think you should get him a suit.

JO-JO: Yeah?

FRED: But you don't have a lot of money.

JO-JO: I know that.

FRED: Are you still makin payments for the kids.

JO-JO: I'm tryin. I been tryin. 6 years, yo. It's a long time. It's been like financially drainin.

PROMOTER: Yeah . . .

FRED: 19 . . . 1995.

JO-JO: '94.

*Pause.*

JO-JO: Look at that.

FRED: What happen?

JO-JO: They tore down that ballfield, Freddie.

FRED: Uh?

JO-JO: Look . . .

FRED: What'd they do that for?

JO-JO: I don't know. It looks like they're puttin it under construction.

FRED: Yeah.

JO-JO: Right? De-struction, even.

FRED: Yeah. What are they gonna do though, for the 9 year olds.

JO-JO: You mean the diamonds?

FRED: Yeah.

JO-JO: This year? I don't know. I bet . . . yeah . . . I guess they'll think of something . . . The big question is what are they gonna do about the gym. I mean who are they gonna give that to? They better not give it back to the high school. That would be terrible. You saw what they did with that. They did that with the lounge, even. They saw what could happen once the high schoolers get a hold of it.

*Pause.*

But can you imagine what that musta been like when they built those diamonds? Way back when? The school? Can you imagine how they felt when they finished building that? I don't know.

*Pause.*

Mostly, kids is they have no respect for any program. You know? I mean these kids have video games, they have only games. Let me tell you something. If you want to get technical, these boys have got none of the things we had. They got none of the things Mom and Dad had, even.

FRED: Like what? I think they got tons of stuff.

JO-JO: Like what . . . Look around you. —They do have tons of stuff. Too much stuff.

FRED: That's what I'm telling you.

JO-JO: Fred, when Mommy was a kid it was like she had to go out to the farm to get her milk. It was like a farm, yo. They had it and they would milk it in the morning and bring it in and the people like Ma come in for the milk and the milk was still warm from that morning. So . . . That was a long time ago, but it wasn't that long ago.

FRED: Who knew that?

JO-JO: Who knew that. I knew that. You're younger. You didn't know my mom. I knew Mommy and I remember it.

FRED: I know. I know.

JO-JO: But I'm sayin that think how much things have changed since then. It's like all games, now. Everybody's playin games. That's all.

FRED: Yeah.

JO-JO: I get so sad thinking about Mommy and when I think about her I get depressed. She was a good person and she taught me well, she taught me a lot, and I appreciate that and maybe you didn't get that Freddie, and I'm not saying you're different than me—

FRED: No—

JO-JO: But that what she taught me, you didn't get so you don't have to think you have a disadvantage—

FRED: No—

JO-JO: I don't mean that, but I mean—Dad did all he could, but she left him a load with me. And you—I see these kids and they're running around cuttin everybody's head off and—

FRED: No—

JO-JO: AND, and I think about how much crap they get and I KNOW how much crap you have to deal with. And I'm just saying people want this and they want that and they'll do anything to get it and then they get it and they don't want it anymore, even! . . .

FRED: Yeah.

JO-JO: I'm yeah—I'm basically looking for that one moment of good well, of peace and good well-being between people. And then it can go. That's all. But I haven't found that. You know? And that's what keeps me going . . . You know?

FRED: Yeah.

JO-JO: Yeah. *(Sings)* "And I still haven't found what I'm looking for . . ."

FRED: Ha ha ha . . .

*Pause.*

PROMOTER: I know what you're talkin about Jo-Jo.

JO-JO: Yeah.

*Pause.*

You wanna see the gym?

FRED: Uh?

JO-JO: No. Promoter—you wanna see the gym?

FRED: Oh.

PROMOTER: Yeah, I do. Do you have keys?

JO-JO: Okay. We'll go in a little while . . .

*Pause.*

Fred, did you work yesterday?

FRED: No. Did you?

JO-JO: Oh, yeah. I forgot. You got fired. Ahhhhhhh!! *(Points at Fred)*

FRED: Awwww.

JO-JO: No, I'm jokin.

FRED: Shut up. It's true, though.

JO-JO: I know but I'm still jokin little brother.

FRED: You would, anyway.

PROMOTER: Did you get fired?

JO-JO: Yeah he did.

FRED:

PROMOTER: I'm sorry about that, Fred.

FRED: Why? You didn't do it.

JO-JO: Did you hear about Stevo, though?

FRED: No.

JO-JO: He was looking for a room number . . . And was like—I'm looking for 387. Does anyone know where 387 is? Oh yeah. 387. Angelo? Do you know where's 387?

FRED: Uh-oh.

JO-JO: You know? Hah! Where's 387? 387 East Building. First of all, this guy doesn't know where 387 East Building is. And Angelo says, "I know where 387 is." Stevo goes, "Where is it?" Angelo's thinkin, Why are you not with the other job in West Building where I told you to go? But no, Angelo goes, "387. 387 . . . Okay. I think I know where that is." And Angelo goes—'cause he knew Stevo was supposed to be on the other job in 113 and he's . . . he goes —"This is 387." Ha! You know? He's telling him that the room is 387 . . . Hah! You know. Stevo: "I can't find it! I can't find it!" He's lookin for the number . . . Hah hah hah! Angelo says, "Jimmy's in there. Did you knock?" Stevo: "Yeah I knocked. I was banging. The guy wasn't in there." Then Brett comes out: "Where's my phone? Where's my phone? Is that my phone?" All this. "Did FedEx come?" All this . . . you know?! And Stevo is like: "I don't know where the hell is 387!" Brett is like: "What's the problem over there?" You know because he's Vice-Principal now. Nobody answers. Angelo's cryin! Stevo is like: "I was banging! I kept kickin and I fucked-up my foot." Yeah! . . . Hah hah hah. "Where's 387!!" And Angelo keeps sayin, "That's it! That's 387!!" Hah! Hah haa!

FRED: Hah ha ha!
JO-JO: Ha ha ha haah!

*Pause.*

FRED: We should start shoutin: "Stevo sucks!" Remember?
JO-JO: Yeah!
ALL: Stevo sucks! Stevo sucks! Hah hah hah!!
JO-JO: Promoter, do you know this guy?
PROMOTER: Huh? I think I do.
FRED: . . . Oh . . . whoa . . . oh ohh ohhh . . . I can't believe that
    . . . that's so funny . . .

*Pause.*

PROMOTER: How you feelin today, Freddie.
FRED: Uh?
PROMOTER: You feelin good?
FRED: I feel okay. I feel okay.
JO-JO: What's a matter? You too tired?
FRED: Yeah. Maybe I'm too tired.
JO-JO: You might feel better later, though. I know lotta times,
    I feel that.
PROMOTER: Fred? You gonna be ready for the fight?

*Pause.*

FRED *(Sees something)*: . . . Ohh, shit, look at this guy . . .

*Pause.*

PROMOTER: Fred? You gonna be ready for the fight?
FRED: I don't know.
PROMOTER: C'mon! What would you rather be doing?
FRED: Oh, man, I can think of tons of stuff I'd rather be doing.
PROMOTER: Like what?
JO-JO: Like goin over to Marissa's house right now . . .

FRED: Awww . . .

JO-JO: Marissa!! I love you!

FRED: Awww. Shut up.

JO-JO: Maybe if Fred isn't gonna start in with his comments like yesterday, then we get along and have a fight. But, if he's gotta say somethin smart . . . Ahhh?

FRED: What happen?

JO-JO: Nothin—I'm talkin about what happened yesterday. That was a mess.

FRED: What happen yesterday?

JO-JO: Nothin. It's not a big thing.

FRED: What?

JO-JO: No, you had to say somethin smart and we were workin, Promoter.

FRED: What I say?

JO-JO: Forget it.

FRED: Tell me, Jo-Jo. What'd I do?

PROMOTER: Fred?

JO-JO: Hey, like you were sayin how you just copy me. You were bein smart.

FRED: No, I didn't. I do copy you. That's what I do. 'Cause you know how to do it.

JO-JO: That's okay. Forget it.

FRED: No, you had lotta fights . . . Jo-Jo.

JO-JO: Forget it then, but we were workin and tryin and I thought you were laughin at me. You were laughin at me. I thought you were makin jokes.

FRED: I wasn't laughin at you. This guy is so sensitive.

JO-JO: Drop it, Fred.

FRED: Quit actin like a woman. Damn . . .

JO-JO: What'd I say?

*Pause.*

PROMOTER: The school board had a meeting yesterday. They weren't going to let me use the gym, because they just used money to fix it up, but I talked to them and got them to let me use the gym. You know? They had to vote and they granted us use of the gym.

JO-JO: For real?

PROMOTER: That's what I'm telling you.

JO-JO: Didn't I hook you up? Didn't I tell you? Ohhh.

PROMOTER: And I can't make up the flyers for this until I know for sure who's gonna be on this card. So, Freddie. You gotta let me know for sure. You know? If I can make up flyers there's an associate who will do them at cost. I have another lead on, friend of an old associate, who says he'll take 25 percent off the back door. And I thought that was pretty generous, because he's gonna let us have first crack at it, so his take will be after our take . . . I'm looking for certain people. Certain people. I'm looking for 5 or 6 adventure capitalists who are capable of an adventure this size and scope . . . It shouldn't be too hard to find somebody who gets excited by this. And as soon as I do, the sky's the limit for us.

JO-JO: Fred. You should see the ring now. They put money into fixing the ring. It's better.

FRED: Okay.

JO-JO: You really think we'll make money on this?

PROMOTER: Huh? Depends . . . if television gets involved. Who can say. This is just the beginning. It's exciting. And I'll do my best to make it happen. But you gotta start somewhere. Everything starts somewhere.

JO-JO: Yeah . . .

PROMOTER: But I gotta get the schools and community behind this, and when I do I want you guys to be ready, that's really important.

JO-JO: Yeah . . . We'll be ready. Right, Fred?

*Pause.*

What am I gonna get for Dad, though. I don't have any ideas. I'm terrible at this, yo . . . shopping.

*They walk.*

*(To Fred)* I liked that fight last night, Fred. He really knew
what to do? Jamie. You know that? He was readin that, even.
So smooth and simple. I like to think that fight wasn't fixed,
but you never know. Monkey business. Monkey business?
FRED: Yeah.

*Pause.*

JO-JO: Promoter, let's go see the gym now.
PROMOTER: Do you have keys?
JO-JO: Do I have keys? *(He shakes keys)* You wanna go over
    there? Let's go. You wanna come, Freddie?
FRED: Uh? No. I'm gonna go to Marissa's house. I'll walk with
    you, Jo-Jo.
JO-JO: All right, Freddie.
PROMOTER: Come on, champ.

*They walk to Marissa's house. Jo-Jo and Promoter follow
Fred, then exit.*

# 2

*Marissa's House.*

FRED: Whaddya doin? . . . Uh? . . . Where's your sister? . . . Uh?
    Is your sister in there? Is she in there? . . . little man . . .
    Uh? . . .

*Marissa enters.*

Let me in . . . Let me in! . . . Open up . . . Where is she? . . .
C'mon . . . Let me in.

MARISSA: Hello, Fred!

FRED: What happen? Marissa!

MARISSA: What do you want?

FRED: Nothin. What are you doin?

MARISSA: I was talkin to my sister.

FRED: Oh yeah. What's goin on? —Oh my God. *(He grabs her)*

MARISSA: Stop it.

FRED: I was just seein how you were doing.

MARISSA: That's nice. I don't like rain.

FRED: Yeah . . . It's been a while.

MARISSA: Not really.

FRED: Yeah.

FRED: So what are you doin?

MARISSA: I'm babysitting.

FRED: Yeah?

MARISSA: Yeah.

FRED: So, what's goin on? Come here.

MARISSA: Nothin.

FRED: Can I come in?

MARISSA: No. Did you work today?

FRED: How come?

MARISSA: I don't want you to.

FRED: Really?

MARISSA: It's really true.

FRED: Well, oh my God . . . *(He grabs her again)*

MARISSA: Stop. What's goin on.

FRED: What are you working on?

MARISSA: Nothing. Did you work today, I said.

FRED: Nah.

MARISSA: Did you have fun with Lisa dancing?

FRED: Nah. I'm not with her anymore. She's—

MARISSA: Why not?

FRED: She's always so back and forth anyway. I'm tired of that.

MARISSA: I thought you said you liked her.

FRED: She has a nice body. Big tits, big ass. You know? More
than a handful.

MARISSA: Fred.

FRED: What? It's true!

MARISSA: I believe you.

FRED: Ha ha. I don't know. Where were you yesterday?

MARISSA: New Jersey. Anita's grandparents are sick and I went out there to see her.

FRED: Hey. I think I gotta job.

MARISSA: Yeah? God bless you.

FRED: Yeah. I think I'm gonna fight.

MARISSA: Really? What happened at the school?

FRED: Come on. Come here . . . *(Grabs her again)*

MARISSA: No. I'm busy and my sister's here.

FRED: Come on. Please?

MARISSA: How's your father?

FRED: He's good. It's his birthday. C'mon . . . *(His hands on her)* Let me feel your titties.

MARISSA: Sweetie you're touching me an awful lot.

FRED: Aww . . . Can't I just talk to you?

MARISSA: We are talking . . .

FRED: Inside, though. Please?

MARISSA: Come here . . . *(She kisses him)*

FRED: So let me tell you—I'm gonna fight.

MARISSA: What's that? 500 bucks?

FRED: No. It's more if I win.

MARISSA: Don't be embarrassed.

FRED: I'm not jokin!

MARISSA: I'm not laughing.

FRED: And it's more if I win.

MARISSA: And how does that feel?

FRED: Uh?

MARISSA: How does that feel?

FRED: How does that feel? How does what feel?

MARISSA: It's a simple question. How do you feel?

FRED: I don't know! I don't know what you're talkin about half the time.

MARISSA: You can't tell me what you feel like?

FRED: I feel like coming inside.

MARISSA: See, that's what you feel like. That's good. Now you know.

FRED: Why? What do you feel like?

MARISSA: I feel like I'm gonna disappoint you.

FRED: Awwww. You would anyway . . .

MARISSA: It's okay. *(Pause)* Come on. You'll get wet. Come inside.

*Fred and Marissa exit.*


## 3

*The party before the fight. Jo-Jo and Promoter enter, Jo-Jo pushes a keg.*

PROMOTER: Jo-Jo, look at what people will give their time to as they go through life . . . When you're young, they give time to things like going out, havin a good time and partying, but they don't give a lot of time to things like retirement, health, thinkin about dying, you know, people don't want to think about dying or their faith too much when they young, but as you grow older, you get wiser, you start to think about these things and the things that didn't used to be important become important. What you start to see is a shift that happens through your life that starts with thinking about things that are about havin fun and what not, and then it shifts as you grow and grow, and that big conclusion starts to emerge and you see that you aren't always going to be this way this young, this fit. So your values change, and as the picture changes the value changes along. This is your life span. This, is a life span theory.

JO-JO: And people are livin a lot longer than they were. People live a long-ass time, now. Can you imagine what it must

have been like for people a 100 years ago? It seems like a
long time ago, but when you think about it, it really isn't.
Think about how people had to work, how they had to live,
and it was like they would live, 40 years, 30 years. They didn't
live that long, even . . .

*Fred enters.*

PROMOTER: Mm-hm. Here's an example. Look. Fred.
FRED: What happen?
PROMOTER: Freddie, have you ever invested anything? . . .
FRED: Uhh . . . I play Lotto.
JO-JO: Hahh! Tell you what. Come by my office tomorrow and
we can talk about some of this! Can you do that?
FRED: You don't have an office.
JO-JO: Yeah, yeah . . . I know what you're saying. 'Cause I see in
my life like 5 years ago. I didn't think about where was the
money gonna come from, but now I look at that more and
more. I mean like with Fred. I keep thinking about it an'
I look at him and I'm like, that's my little brother and
I wanna see him get the chances. Maybe he gets the chances
I didn't get. That's all. Right, Fred?
PROMOTER: A lot of people, anyone can look in the past and see
5 years ago—but who can see 5 years into the future? Who?
Nobody. Can Fred? People would be foolish to think that
anyone can predict the future. You can't predict the future.
You can't say what's gonna happen. And if you're right,
you're a genius, right? But if you're wrong, you're a fool. So
I'm not gonna say that I can see what the future has in store,
but I am gonna say that anything, ANYTHING—can happen. And you need to be ready for anything. Ready for anything to happen. That's the smartest thing you can do . . . Be
ready for anything.
JO-JO: Actually, I'm really scared about what's gonna happen.
I'm not like thinking about it or whatever, but I have
thought about it.

PROMOTER: My man Freddie plays the lottery every day and
     that's like his insurance. He really thinks that he's gonna hit
     it. He got his numbers, he got his system, but I look at him
     and I'm like—I just feel sad. I look at him, and I'm like,
     you—you don't have any idea how stupid this is. You're
     never gonna win. You need to take that money and put it
     somewhere where it can do something. I mean—buy stocks
     or something, don't put your money into Lotto, and DON'T
     tell me you're investing in something 'cause you're not
     investing in things. You throwin it away.
FRED: Awwww, this guy's a pain in the ass. Really.
PROMOTER: Serious. I like to give an overview of a situation and
     an overview to people and I like to know where they've been
     and then I can tell them what all the options are. First of all,
     the situation as it stands right now is pointing to something
     very significant. The tech. And all this new technology has
     created an unprecedented situation, and it's going to
     change the way we see the world and the world is going to
     look very different than it did for our parents, your parents.
     But the change is inevitable. You can agree with this or not
     agree with it. But this is the future. I like where it's headed.
     I mean it's kind of a techno-y thing but it doesn't get annoy-
     ing. And I can tell you that I invest myself. I invest for me
     and I invest for my kids' sake too. I can read the current sit-
     uation and I can see, "Yeah, this is where it's headed.
     Therefore, I'm going to go this way." And that's the ticket.
     People like to say it's brain surgery or rocket science but it
     isn't. But are you a child? You're not a child. If you have
     monsters in the shadows you could be afraid of the dark.
     Are you afraid of the dark? Just invest or whatever.
FRED: Is this what you learned in college?
PROMOTER: Huh? Yeah. Some of it.
FRED: What you mean though about it going somewhere? Goin
     into what? Where do you put it?
PROMOTER: Whatever. Put it into things.
FRED: What is it.

PROMOTER: Whatever you want.

FRED: No, but what is it? What are you doing?

PROMOTER: Huh? I put it into stocks and things. I have mutual fund, retirement, I got life . . . you'll see what I mean. But put it away. Don't spend it. I gotta pee.

*Promoter exits. Pause.*

JO-JO: What's goin on Fred?

FRED: I don't know. I'm thinking a lot about what was said just now by him. You know what he said was true.

JO-JO: Yeah but he took so long . . . nobody takes that long to say something. That's what college is.

FRED: What are you drinking?

JO-JO: Tangerine.

FRED: Awwh!

JO-JO: Ohh! Yeah? What?

FRED: That stuff's nasty.

JO-JO: No . . . You think?

FRED *(Sees someone)*: Look . . .

JO-JO: That's cool.

FRED: I think it was true what he said.

JO-JO: Yeah that's what school is. That's how you learn. You go to school.

FRED: You wanna go to college ever?

JO-JO: College? Who's goin to college?

FRED: Nobody.

JO-JO: Look. There she is.

FRED: The one from—ohh! Is that her?

JO-JO: Yeah. I think so . . . So young.

FRED: Too young. Too young for you.

JO-JO: If there's grass on the field, play ball, yo.

FRED: Ha. That's stupid.

JO-JO: Is Marissa comin?

FRED: She said she was. She better. I hope she is.

JO-JO: All right. All right . . . Hey. If you don't love her, I will. Remember that.

FRED: I wouldn't mind goin to college, Jo-Jo.

JO-JO: Now?

FRED: I don't know. I mean, I might, but I haven't made up my mind yet.

*Promoter enters.*

JO-JO: Yeah, well first of all you need to get the grades. If you don't have the grades you might as well SIT DOWN SON!

FRED: No no I know. But the people who go, what's it like?

JO-JO: Oh, I don't know.

FRED: Didn't you go?

JO-JO: That was technical college. You should ask Promoter.

PROMOTER: What?

FRED: When you go away some place to college. How to get in.

PROMOTER: Oh! They have other concerns too. Like whether you were in the certain rank in school. And outside activities like charities and the like. Sports. That all figures in.

FRED: But what is it like? What is college like?

PROMOTER: Well, it's a lot of fun. A lot of the social skills that I learned I learned in college and those social skills I wouldn't have picked up anywhere else. And the people I met there are still some of my closest contacts. And the social life is great. I met a lot of great-looking girls there. And it's great because you can do anything you want. I felt like anything was possible.

JO-JO: Is it true they have to get you a Big Brother.

FRED: What's that?

PROMOTER: What?

JO-JO: Big Brother?

FRED: What is that?

PROMOTER: You know that?

JO-JO: Yeah . . .

PROMOTER: For Greek fraternities. Fraternities—

FRED: Oh oh oh oh oh. I know what you're talking about.

PROMOTER: You have to get a Big Brother.

FRED: I know what you're talking about.

PROMOTER: I mean you get a Big Brother.

FRED: Yeah. I know exactly what you're talking about.

JO-JO: Yeah, he knows what a Big Brother is.

FRED: Would I get to pick a Big Brother?

JO-JO: No. They pick it.

FRED: How do they know who will be the Big Brother.

PROMOTER: They do. It was chosen for me.

JO-JO: For real?

PROMOTER: Yeah.

JO-JO: I didn't know. You know? I never thought about it. But they get to pick it. Okay.

*Pause.*

PROMOTER: Are you guys having a good time at this party?

FRED AND JO-JO: Yeah . . .

PROMOTER: Are you ready Fred?

*Marissa enters.*

FRED: Marissa!

MARISSA: Hi Freddie!

FRED: What.

MARISSA: Hey, Jo-Jo. *(To Promoter)* Hello. *(To Fred)* C'mon, Freddie. Let's get things started.

FRED: No, I don't wanta dance.

MARISSA: What'sa matter?

FRED: No, I don't wanta dance.

MARISSA: Jo-Jo?

JO-JO: No, thanks. I might want to later.

MARISSA: Well, there's nothing wrong with dancing. I'm gonna dance myself.

FRED: Go ahead!

*Marissa dances.*

MARISSA: I think it's funny how you all are boxers and you won't
dance.

*Pause.*

FRED: I'm gonna dance . . .

*Fred hands Jo-Jo his drink cup. Jo-Jo and Promoter exit.*

Please . . . look. I got something for you . . .
MARISSA: What is it?
FRED: Open it . . . It's a ring.
MARISSA: Where'd you get this? Sol's?
FRED: Next to Sol's.
MARISSA: Oh.
FRED: Do you like it?
MARISSA: I like it. It's sweet.
FRED: Well . . . Are you gonna answer me?
MARISSA: What's the question?
FRED: Well, you know what I mean.
MARISSA: You can't ask?
FRED: Yeah, I can . . .
MARISSA: Do you have a plan?
FRED: Plan? What are you talkin about?
MARISSA: What is it. Tell me what the plan is.
FRED: . . . Get married.
MARISSA: That's not a plan, Federíco.
FRED: Why not?
MARISSA: I'm sorry, Fred. But I realized something. I didn't see
it before. You have to look inside yourself and tell me what's
in your heart. That's the only way we can see this whole
thing. You have to be honest with me and if you can be hon-
est with me you can be honest with yourself. Please listen
to me. You have to look into your heart and the answer is

there, all the answers are there. Can you do that, Fred?
I can. I'm willing to try. I need you to take a moment and
look at what's around you and take into account everything
and look, look around you. There's a well deep inside you
and this is what you have to realize. That the answer is
there. You have to go in and find it. Do you know? I have
seen the truth now. Oh, I feel so much bigger now that
I have seen the truth. I know what to do and this is so much
better than you or me. I'm talking about something that
puts things in their proper place. I'm talking about, I'm talking about how I found something and I can't say what that
is except that it feels close to God. That's what I feel and
that's what it has to be because I've never felt like this.
—Oh, I've lied to you before and I know you've lied to me
but I don't want this. I don't want to do this to you anymore.
I don't want to do that to anyone . . . Fred. This is what
I want from you. This is what I'm going to do. I found this
place and I want to go there. Please, Federíco, please. I'm
not tired anymore, I'm not afraid anymore, I'm just realizing what I've seen. I've only seen these things in dreams
before, in my dreams, I looked for them in dreams, now
I see them. I never understood them until now. Now I see . . .
FRED: . . . What happen?
MARISSA: I'm sorry. It's all my fault.

*Pause.*

Okay? . . .
FRED: Forget it.

*Fred takes ring back.*

MARISSA: No, I won't forget it. I'm never going to forget this.
I swear it.
FRED: Forget I asked you.
MARISSA: You never did ask me Freddie.

FRED: Yeah . . .

MARISSA: But if this is good-bye then I want us to be honest with each other and then at least we can have a good time together . . . Here, dance with me.

FRED: No, I don't think so.

MARISSA: Come here.

*They dance.*

FRED: . . . All these girls are lookin at me.

*Fred exits. Marissa exits.*

# 4

*The fight. Jo-Jo and Promoter enter.*

JO-JO: . . . My hands are sweaty. Yo, I hate that.

PROMOTER:

*Jo-Jo pulls a urinal cake out of his pocket.*

JO-JO: You ever see one of these?

PROMOTER: What's that?

*Jo-Jo holds it out. Promoter shakes his head.*

JO-JO: See?

PROMOTER: What is that?

JO-JO: Weird, right?

PROMOTER: Yeah.

JO-JO: It's like outer space, right?

PROMOTER:

JO-JO: It's for . . .

PROMOTER: Oh yeah, exactly.

JO-JO: Ha ha ha. *(Pushes Promoter)*

*Jo-Jo checks the door.*

It's not open . . .

PROMOTER: I thought you had keys.

JO-JO: I did. I forgot em.

PROMOTER: Joe?

JO-JO: These guys are all working here . . . Somebody's got keys.

PROMOTER: Do you know this fighter?

JO-JO: Who. Yeah, I know him. I think I know him. How do you know him.

PROMOTER: Huh? I worked with early education.

JO-JO: Okay . . . okay.

*Kid enters.*

PROMOTER: Hey, Ha ha ha! Here's the kid . . . How you doin, Kid?

KID: Gimme back my mow-oo-jo!! Very well, very well.

PROMOTER: All right? Hey, it's the kid. How you doin, champ? Where were you?

KID: What happen?

PROMOTER: I tried calling you.

KID: When?

PROMOTER: Last night. What were you doin?

KID: I was doin laundry.

PROMOTER: Haaah!

KID: I was! I was doin laundry with old ladies. Would you believe it? I was out late. I got home at 8 o'clock in the morning. Huh? I couldn't sleep so I went and did laundry. I was trashed with these old ladies doing my laundry on Sunday morning . . . All right. 8 o'clock in the morning. Where were you at?

PROMOTER: I was up and about.

KID: . . . Oh yeah? How was this party?

PROMOTER: Too much alcohol! . . . yeah.

KID: I heard what's her name came over there.

PROMOTER: Yes.

KID: She's hot.

PROMOTER: Yeah.

KID: But I don't know. I got a vibe from her that she was with Chris Sullivan. I don't know, man. That's my—yeah . . . What are you doing tonight? I don't know. See a movie or something?

PROMOTER: Come with me.

KID: Oh yeah?

PROMOTER: Come out with me and Jessica.

KID: No way.

PROMOTER: Why not!

KID: . . . 'Cause. I'm not going with you.

PROMOTER: Why?

KID: 'Cause . . . No, I'm not going with you and her. That's a date. That's corny. But what are you all doing before?

PROMOTER: We'll be at my house.

KID: Oh yeah? Maybe I'll swing by before . . . You got any video tapes over there? No I thought I'd come over and just shoot the shit or whatever. All right man.

PROMOTER: Yeah. This is Jo-Jo. He's the one I was talkin about.

KID: We're gonna make money on this one.

JO-JO: Yeah?

KID: I'm askin.

JO-JO: Oh, I thought you were telling me.

KID: Well, are we?

PROMOTER: Yeah.

KID: We like the sound of that.

PROMOTER: Well, don't count your chickens.

JO-JO: Oh, so we're not gonna make money.

PROMOTER *(Laughs)*: No. No. No. It's gonna be good. Right, Kid?

KID: Yeah, yeah . . .

*Fred enters.*

PROMOTER: I'm glad to hear that. I have big expectations for this fight. I myself am really looking forward to it.
JO-JO: It's about time.

*The Ref enters.*

REF: Where are your fighters?
PROMOTER: Right here.
JO-JO: I told Fred that what happened to Stevo. Right, Promoter? Do you know Stevo?
KID: Who?
PROMOTER: Yeah, I liked that.

*Ref unlocks the door. Jo-Jo opens the door. The ring is pushed out by Afleck and Corner.*

JO-JO: Look at this place. How old is this place? This school. This gym. I've been here for 13 years and that feels like forever, but this place has been here forever. Can you imagine how they felt when they built this? There's a lot of history here. You can feel it. A lot of history.
PROMOTER: Fred, this is Jerry . . .
FRED: How you doin.
KID: Oh my God. You're a lot more frightening in person.

*Pause.*

FRED: So . . . Did you like that fight last night?
KID: Yeah.
FRED: I liked it.
KID: They had a debate.
FRED: Yeah? He wasn't disqualified.
KID: I never said he was. Stop crying about it.
FRED: Oh.

KID: WBC said he was supposed to be a WBC champion, but WBA said he wasn't champ. They had a debate.

FRED: . . . IBO, IBC?

KID: Huh?

FRED: I thought it was IBC.

KID: NO! Now I'm looking at this division and what's gonna happen to this fight. 'Cause if those are the rules, this fight doesn't mean anything. I wonder what they're gonna say. Even if you could possibly beat me, it won't mean anything.

FRED: Yeah?

KID: Yeah. I mean I've seen this a thousand times, a thousand times. It comes down to this: where the commission is in the dark, like this—just like this fight, until it's too late. A 1,000 times. But we don't care about that, do we puny? Huh!? Do we!? AGH!

*Kid pushes Fred. Fred pushes Kid back. All laugh.*

REF: Quiet! Shut yer mouth! Weigh-in! Weigh in! Do you want to be disqualified? Huh? . . . There'll be no talking allowed in this room during the weigh-in. Weigh-in . . . I'm the boss now.

*They weigh-in.*

180 pounds . . . 200 pounds . . .

*Marissa enters. Ref at the microphone:*

REF: Paul, come up here.

PROMOTER: All right, Blue! . . . Welcome to the fight. We have a great fight lined up. Please know that these fighters have trained a long time for this fight and they are going to give it their all. I will be watching the fight from down here, but I will also tell Blue to call the fight if somebody is really hurt bad. Yes, we have quite a fight lined up for this evening. I want to thank all of you for coming. Now this fight wouldn't be possible for me if it weren't for a few key players, so please show your support. If this ring wasn't here, we wouldn't be able to have these events, so please continue to support these events . . . The program has been a continuation of the school board in cooperation with the community and this is all about joint usage. And we thank the kids and the parents just like we thank the fighters, and the promoters. This gym was moved here so the youngsters are now able to utilize this facility again. They were without this ring for many years, they don't remember it ever being here. But I look out at all the fathers here and I know they remember. But this fight I hope draws attention to the need and how a community can share the value and resources that exist here. And that they exist for everyone. And we can celebrate together its return to its proper place. So . . . let's get set for fighting!!!

*Bells.*

Let me start by introducing the fighters to you . . . *(Holds card)* In this corner, at 6 feet, weighing 180 pounds, the king of his boro, El Rey, Federíco Martinez!! . . . In this other corner . . . This man, weighing 200 pounds, 6 feet 2 inches tall, Old Kid Hansen!! Fighters, good luck to both of you.

*Promoter exits the ring.*

MARISSA: Freddie. Listen to me. Fred. Listen. Fred, I know you are hearing this. I also know that you don't want to hear this. Don't fight. Don't fight him. You're gonna get hurt. It's not worth it. You can find something beautiful. You can find it. I know you can! I love you, Fred. I always will love you.
FRED: Yeah . . .
JO-JO: Marissa! Come on! We don't have time for this. This is Fred. Leave him alone.

MARISSA: . . . I love you too, Jo-Jo. Good-bye.

*Bells. Marissa exits.*

REF *(To fighters)*: Come here . . . Listen to me. No messing around. When I say break, you break. You got it, fuckers? . . . Listen to my commands at all times, protect yourselves at all times. If you don't break it up I'm going to take punches away. No joke. You know the rules. Good boxing. Good luck to both of you. Put your gloves up. Put your gloves up.

*The fighters go to their corners. Bell.*
*Round 1.*

JO-JO: No, that's not right . . . No, Fred . . . I do it different . . .
REF *(To Fred)*: What's the matter with you?
PROMOTER: I like it better when you punch each other.

*Bell. End Round 1.*
*Dad enters.*

JO-JO: Fred. Look.
FRED: Uh?
JO-JO: Look! Look who it is. It's Dad, even.
DAD: It's not good enough!!!
JO-JO: Oh! . . .
FRED: Yeah?
DAD: Jo-Jo! Jo-Jo! Mira, esta no es suficiente. You gotta fight harder! ¡Entiende! . . . This guy's gotta month on you.
FRED: Dad, it's me. Freddie.
JO-JO: This is Freddie. I'm Joe, Dad.
DAD: Listen . . . You've got skills, yeah you got skills. You're fast. You're a natural. Pero esto es nuevo. It's raw. I want you to decide something . . . I need you to decide something. I need you to take initiative. If you decide that this is what you want to do, then this is how it's going to be. If you decide,

you will be the greatest fighter . . . No hay duda. Tu seras campeón. Yo te voy a hacer campeón.

JO-JO: Let's go . . . Dad. I'm doing it. Let me do it.

*Bell. Round 2.*
   *Bell. End Round 2.*

DAD: All right, son . . . all right . . . It's all right. I told you . . . Mi hijo, mira . . . Stop this. This is nothing. Get inside. Fight harder. What happens if you quit now—nothing! We go home. Fight harder! You can't turn back! Go! Go! Go! Okay?

FRED: Okay!! Shut up! All right!? This is for me. I don't want to help you! Yeah?! It's me! I'm in the ring! It's for me! Stop! Just stop! Shut up! Get outta my face. Get the fuck out t'way. I'm tired . . . you can on home. Go on home. Gimme back my mouthpiece.

JO-JO: Dad, come on . . .

DAD: Go!!

*Bell. Round 3.*

FRED *(To Kid)*: Come on!!

PROMOTER: That's better.

*Bell. The fight ends. The microphone is lowered.*

Well, the judges are tallying . . . We're just waiting here . . . Uhh . . . Let's see . . .

*Pause. Afleck hands him a card, a trophy.*

PROMOTER: It took a long time for the decision *(Reads the card, shows it to Ref)*

REF: Come on . . . In general, you fought well. There are some things you need to work on, but congratulations. You should both feel good about how you fought . . . This guy's the winner.

PROMOTER: No. Ref. Wait . . . All right . . . Ladies and gentlemen
. . . by a split-decision, the winner: Federíco Martinez!!

AFLECK: Lucky shot.

DAD: Relax . . . You can train and you think that's enough. But
that's not enough. It's never enough. And the other guy's
always got more. More money. More time. And there are
many things you rely on to keep you moving. But you have
to keep moving. Let me tell you something. It is a test of
who you are. Are you brave. Are you excellent. Can you
make it? Vamos a ver lo que tu haces. Y como lo haces.

FRED: Yeah . . . Thanks, Dad.

JO-JO: Dad! It's over. Freddie won. Congratulations, Freddie.
I think you fought really good.

FRED: Thanks . . . Where's Marissa?

JO-JO: I don't know. She was here. I thought I saw her take off.

FRED: Maybe she went home.

JO-JO: Maybe she wants you to go over there . . .

FRED: Yeah, maybe . . .

*Promoter and Jo-Jo exit, followed by Ref and Kid. Fred watches
as the rest exit. Dad stays with Fred for a minute. The ring is
pushed back by Afleck and Corner.*

CORNER: Watch your head, guy.

FRED: Yeah . . . Marissa?! Marissa? . . . Where is she?! . . . Man,
she ain't here . . .

*Door is shut.
    Promoter enters, sings:*

PROMOTER:

> When you're takin it in
> What's the worst thing that can happen
> Well just Big Bird or Jamie Levin
> Get mad at me
> Slip a cap in me

These guys go toe to toe every time
I had 13 fights, I got mine
It ain't panty hose
Or messin around
Goin toe to toe
Round after round

People ask me how it's done
Gamblin on a buck-toothed son-of-a-gun
I'm a gambler
And a rambler
Smoke a little bit
Get a little lit
Don't fuck with me
I'll smack you down
Don't mess with me
I'll take you out.

# 5

*Jo-Jo and Promoter are talking.*

PROMOTER: You know. I think that all in all, it wasn't too bad a
    night. I made some money, you made some money, we
    should talk now about what to do with it. That's the key.
    What you do with it. But it was a great evening, right?
    Where's Freddie.
JO-JO: Not sure. Maybe he's workin. I hope he comes by, I want
    to talk to him about Marissa.
PROMOTER: I thought he got laid off.
JO-JO: He didn't get laid off. He got fired. But he was supposed
    to go in and talk to them to get his job back. He'll get it back.
    They always take him back. It's funny. They work him hard,

then he works hard, too hard, because that's who he is, and then he gets mad and doesn't show up, sleeps late. They call him up and they all yell at him, he quits, or they fire him—and then wait a few months, he's back again. Start all over again. It's funny, even.

*Fred enters.*

PROMOTER: Here he is.

JO-JO: There he is. What's going on? Where's Marissa?

FRED: I don't know.

JO-JO: 'Cause I was thinking about what she said. Yo, what was that?

FRED: Yeah.

JO-JO: And I think she's right. I think she's talkin about sort of what I was talkin about before. I was laughin at it when she said it, but it makes sense. And that little girl's got big balls, even. I want to find that one pure moment, too. Of like understanding. You know? And then it can go. As long as I have that one moment. I can go, too . . . I don't know. I guess it's hard. I imagine it musta been easier way back when.

FRED: Yeah, maybe.

JO-JO: But what happen?

FRED: Whaddya mean?

JO-JO: Well, where is she?

FRED: I told you, I don't know. She's gone.

JO-JO: Oh, man, that's rough. What are you gonna do?

FRED: I don't know.

JO-JO: Keep fighting?

FRED: Keep working. I'll figure it out.

PROMOTER: I can help. If you'll let me.

JO-JO: Are you nuts . . . This guy pays 500. It'd be better if we got nothin, 'cause then we wouldn't relax, and we'd keep workin and at least it would be dignified, like community service or somethin—right, Promoter?

PROMOTER: Well, do you wanna give me my money back?

JO-JO: No, that's not the point.

FRED: Shut up, Jo-Jo.

JO-JO: No, Promoter gonna keep us busy. Right?

*Pause.*

FRED: Promoter. Was that fight fixed?

PROMOTER: Huh? No.

JO-JO: That's fine. Set it up. Keep settin it up. Right, Fred?

FRED: Yeah.

JO-JO: . . . Look. I bought something for Dad.

*Jo-Jo shows Fred gifts.*

FRED: Ohh . . .

JO-JO: And I got something for my kids, too. What do you think
   of that?

FRED: Yeah. Nice.

JO-JO: Come here little brother. It's okay . . .

*They embrace as Promoter joins them.*

JO-JO: Look at that hurricane fence, Fred.

FRED: Yeah, I see that.

JO-JO: I thought they were tearing those diamonds down, but
   they're not. They're making improvements, Fred . . . They're
   not tearing it down. I thought they were tearing it down but
   they're makin it better, even . . . Fred.

FRED: Okay. Yeah. I see that . . .

RICHARD MAXWELL, an Obie Award–winning writer and director, was born in Fargo, ND, and studied acting at Illinois State University. In Chicago, he was a cofounder of the Cook County Theater Department. In 1994 Richard moved to New York and is now the Artistic Director of New York City Players (nycplayers.org).